Speaking Desires can be Dangerous

For Edmond

Speaking Desires can be Dangerous

The Poetics of the Unconscious

Elizabeth Wright

Polity Press

First published in 1999 by Polity Press
in association with Blackwell Publishers Ltd

Editorial office:
Polity Press
65 Bridge Street
Cambridge CB2 1UR, UK

Marketing and production:
Blackwell Publishers Ltd
108 Cowley Road
Oxford OX4 1JF, UK

Published in the USA by
Blackwell Publishers Inc.
Commerce Place
350 Main Street
Malden, MA 02148, USA

ISBN 0-7456-1967-3
ISBN 0-7456-1968-1 (pbk)

A catalogue record for this book is available from the British Library and has been applied for from the Library of Congress.

Typeset in 11 on 13 pt Berling
by Ace Filmsetting Ltd, Frome, Somerset
Printed in Great Britain by TJ International, Padstow, Cornwall

This book is printed on acid-free paper.

Contents

Acknowledgements

My grateful thanks go to the following who have contributed in many ways to my clinical understanding of psychoanalysis: Bernard Barnett, Michael Kennedy, Ian Simpson, Luis Roderiguez de la Sierra, Darian Leader, Vivien Bar and Katrin Stroh. I owe a considerable debt to Wayne Barron for generous time spent in detailed discussion and explication of Lacan. I would also like to thank Kenneth Reinhard, Juliet MacCannell, Danielle Bergeron, Renata Salecil, Slavoj Žižek, Russell Grigg, and my colleagues at Girton for their friendship and support. My greatest debt goes to Edmond Wright, who has participated closely in every stage of the book, from engaging with its structure and argument from a consistent philosophical position to every kind of essential practical help and assistance.

My thanks also go to the following: the Centre for Freudian Analysis and Research for clinical and theoretical knowledge; the staff of Cambridge University Library and Girton College Library for their friendly help in my researches; and the Cambridge University Travel Fund and Girton College for generous financial assistance towards my research expenses.

John Thompson of Polity Press has encouraged the book at all stages from its conception to its final production. The team at Polity Press has given me every possible help, and I should particularly like to thank Julia Harsant for her unfailing friendliness and efficiency, the desk editor, Sue Leigh and the copy editor, Ruth Thackeray, for their generous care and attention.

The publishers wish to thank Gillon Aitken Associates for permission to reprint material from *Spanking the Maid* by Robert Coover © 1982 Robert Coover. They would also like to thank The Grove Press Inc. for permission to reprint material from *Spanking the Maid* by Robert Coover.

Introduction

One of Sigmund Freud's abiding concerns when analysing literature and the arts was the question of who had priority in the discovery of the unconscious, the poet or the psychoanalyst, that is, Freud himself. To touch on a long-standing controversy between literature and psychoanalysis: who understands the unconscious best, the poet or the clinician? Or, to put it another way, do the aesthetic and the clinical have to speak in entirely different languages or does the poetic enter both?

Just as with the advent of modern literary theory it was found 'that there are more things in literary texts than are dreamt of in Freudian philosophy',[1] so there are also many things in literary texts that the critic had not been conscious of before the advent of psychoanalysis. What is more, when some of Freud's writings were themselves read literally, taken at their word, scanned for their slippages and gaps,[2] it became apparent that psychoanalytic texts were no more immune from a literary reading than any other text. The assumption of the authority of psychoanalysis over literature was first properly challenged in an influential volume inaugurating a dialectical exchange between psychoanalysis and literature, where psychoanalysis points to the unconscious of literature and literature to the unconscious of psychoanalysis.[3] If the unconscious has a poetics that invades texts of whatever kind, there can be no secure position inside or outside a text that sustains a reliable meaning.

Some thirty years ago an innovative critic, Wayne C. Booth, did much to enliven and reform a literary criticism that was somewhat moribund even though it had called itself 'New'.[4] In his *The Rhetoric of Fiction* [5] he set out to demonstrate that there was more to rhetoric than rules and regulations and more to literature than canon-formation. Focusing on the conscious and unconscious communicative strategies available to the author – what 'he' (in those days) does to persuade the reader to accept his proffered fictional world – Booth favours the textual illusion of a writer who reliably transmits his norms and values through the creation of an 'implied author': although the real author, like a mother, may come and go, he projects a reliable double into the text (a father?), who, free from any quirkiness, upholds the norms and values the author would like to believe in. If this now sounds a little quaint, it still has considerable practical use in making a first acquaintance with a text, since it has an eye for stable ironic structures.

However, theoretically, Booth's idea of a rhetoric of fiction implies that the dubious distinction between literary/poetic language and scientific/ordinary language can be upheld. But literary theory is really a theory about how all language works and is itself subject to the laws of language: to investigate literature is always, in one way or another, to investigate language. And language is inescapably figural, as the title of this book, *Speaking Desires can be Dangerous*, illustrates. It has the same grammatical ambiguity as Noam Chomsky's notorious sentence, 'Flying planes can be dangerous', with which he was showing how the same sequence of words can have different deep structures. The subject of the sentence, 'Flying planes', can be either a gerund (verbal noun) phrase or a noun modified by a gerundive (verbal adjective). He was thereby demonstrating that surface features are no guide to structure.[6] The ambiguity is nicely illustrated by the title of Ian McEwan's novel *Enduring Love* (1997). Two meanings are similarly derivable from my title: meaning 1 (the gerund), *to speak our desires is dangerous* (since our words do not arrive at the desires we thought we had); meaning 2 (the gerundive), *the desires that are speaking are dangerous* (since they speak of what we do not want to know anything about). My title thus performs what it says, that desire works in the very structure of language. Hence rhetoric has a fictive element. Its effects are enigmatic and incalculable because of the very contingency of what human action has to operate upon in the world. Rhetoric represents a continuing attempt to adjust the order of language to an ever-recalcitrant matter.

Psychoanalytic literary theory has a distinctive contribution to make in this area. From the beginning Freud moved between the discourse of the scientist and that of the artist, the novelist and the poet, availing himself freely of their themes and poetic figures. Both he and his followers paid attention to literature and the arts, taking them to employ the same processes that psychoanalysis uncovered in the workings of the unconscious. Psychoanalysis has a particular theory about why language is literary all the time, a particular way of accounting for the irrepressible figurality of language as it betrays the operations of desire and fantasy: the fact that language is inescapably figural makes equally for the stuff of literature, criticism and psychoanalysis. The issue of poetics is therefore much wider than that of psychoanalysis itself and is reachable without its clinical offices, something that Freud acknowledged in his homage to the poets. Hence this book does not want to suggest that the paradigms of psychoanalysis render all other discourses secondary. Nor that the psychoanalysts treated here are to be seen as self-proclaimed prophets but rather as implicit collaborators free to cancel out one another's excesses.

By the same token, criticism likes to parade itself as a species of meta-language, more knowing than, if poetically inferior to, the language of the writer. This ignores the fact that all language is rhetoric in that it is an act of persuasion, an attempt to shift desires. Rhetoric invariably works on the presupposition of an innocent transference of meaning, that meanings can be transferred without undergoing any change. When talking about 'the rhetoric of fiction' this presupposition is not recognized: if, on the other hand, we were to invert the title into 'the fiction of rhetoric', we recognize that the transference is by no means innocent. What is at stake here is a *reading*, a work of interpretation, in which there is no agreement among subjects as to how this work might be done. The term 'subject' is used throughout this book precisely to acknowledge that to maintain oneself in language brooks of no division between conscious and unconscious. Writer/reader, analyst/analysand are all readers and have to struggle with the failure of language to deliver what it seems to promise. It is the aim of this book to detect the operations of desire by engaging simultaneously with the literary and the clinical, to read the literary with a clinical eye and also the clinical with a literary one.

In Part I, I focus on Freudian psychoanalysis and try to demonstrate the necessity of the clinical/aesthetic interchange. With the example of a well-known nonsense poem by Edward Lear I show how the fundamental fantasies recognized by psychoanalysis are woven into its themes, rhythms and figures. I argue for the presence of sexuality in the text in that what is inscribed is the violation and reinstatement of the Law, uncannily repeated in the form of transgressive fantasies that are induced through the confrontation of author and reader.

This leads me into a discussion of Freud's essay on 'The uncanny', written in 1919, which has become a key epistemological and aesthetic concept in contemporary thought. The uncanny emerges both in the clinical and literary encounter and also in the fragile reality of life. It is precisely when our complacent identities are challenged by the unexpected that the uncanny is experienced: the most familiar and therefore the most reassuring is transformed into the strange. An acknowledgement of the permanent presence of radical otherness thus becomes the central recommendation of psychoanalysis and literature alike, for both their narratives have precisely this feature, that an easy assumption is exposed to subversion by the incalculable. The uncanny (*unheimlich*) can here be linked to Surrealism since both point to the unreliability of sense perception: the familiar world of common objects is rendered 'unhomely' through the invasion of the unconscious. The visual uncanny of Surrealism provides me with a domain that is more rhetorically immediate, a kind of visual aid that enables me to delineate the effects that reappear in literature. I use Freud's example of the 'Wolf Man' in order to provide a clinical demonstration of the uncanny's effects in the life of a patient. In all these examples, those from Surrealism, Freud's own essay and Freud's clinical case, the uncanny breaks through the work of fantasy as it endeavours to hide from the subject both the subject's own inadequacy within the symbolic and the symbolic's inadequacy in mapping the subject and the world.

Alfred Kubin's novel *The Other Side* (1909) , shows what happens when there is an attempt to build up a fantasy of an omnipotent creator who will guarantee the perfect fulfilment of all desires in a dream kingdom. Like the uncanny, fantasy arises at the point where both the object and the symbolic which sustains it fail us, but at the same point the uncanny breaks through. It is only through inquiring into our fantasies that, paradoxically, we can discover what we are trying to hide, the failure of the symbolic to render us complete: the fantasy arises where the subject deludes itself that the symbolic knows what it is supposed to be. The subject is thus trying to install the Law without the price that the Law exacts, as if desire and drive were of one mind. Kubin's text 'knows' that the *reductio ad absurdum* of this delusion is chaos, and it invites the reader into a literary psychosis.

Julia Kristeva's investigations into those 'maladies of the soul' that are peculiar to contemporary life, the so-called 'border-line' disorders, bring together clinical and aesthetic counter-parts of suffering. Within a general theoretical discourse on depression and melancholia she provides both clinical case material and literary and artistic examples that testify to a struggle with mourning. In her clinical material she shows her patients to be wavering between neurosis and psychosis in their attempts to avoid dialogue with the world as it is repre-sented by their analyst and significant figures of their past: to avoid the dialogic nature of speech is to persist in an uncon-scious commitment to suffering as a way of refusing to mourn. The monologic and lifeless language of the depressive subject, which includes both speech and silence, keeps the other at bay so as not to disturb an indwelling on its own grievance rather than to find the way to grief. In the course of the treat-ment the patient's monologue is uncannily disturbed by the

repeated breaking through of the fantasy, as was the case in
the example from Kubin's *The Other Side*. In both the clinical
and aesthetic domains the poetics of the unconscious finds its
way of elaborating the dynamics of 'mourning and melancholia' (Freud) in figurative terms. The refusal to give up the lost
object provides the energy which keeps the depression going;
the drive refuses to divest itself of the maternal encumbrance
and to invest in the substitutions of the symbolic. In the work
of James Joyce and Fyodor Dostoevsky, Kristeva detects two
different poetic resolutions of this common pathology, resulting from two different clinical structures, psychosis and neurosis. In the case of Joyce, a disturbance in language exploits
and holds off an incipient psychosis by simultaneously absorbing in his text the combination of maternal power and
paternal identification that was eluding him in life. In the case
of Dostoevsky, a neurotic suffering which incessantly dwells
on self-punishment is finally resolved through the trope of
forgiveness, whereby the harshness of the Law is reinscribed
and transformed through regaining faith in an originary benevolent parent figure.

In Part II the emphasis shifts from Freud to Jacques Lacan.
Although for Freud language was clearly at the centre of analysis, he was unable to make use of the findings of modern linguistics. In applying linguistics Lacan was able to move
decisively to a position in which language was seen as crucial
to the constitution of the subject. He was thus able to shift
the emphasis from the dialogic nature of language to its structure as a discourse of desire. This involves a series of unstable
positions for all subjects and requires a continual engagement
with Lacan's three orders, the symbolic, the real and the imaginary, his theoretical apparatus for mapping the operations
of desire in language. The symbolic, a word-hoard that is available for every subject that enters it, is at the same time the
occasion for the subject's alienation from its own substantial
being. Its effort to maintain a social bond under such pressure
is charted in Lacan's discourse 'mathemes'. These are formu-
laic models for what happens when the dominant position in
the discourse is occupied by different aspects of the speech
situation, according to whether the status quo is maintained

or challenged. Literature and the arts are the place where this struggle is vicariously fought out: for Lacan art is something that analyses the subject (for instance, his reading of Edgar Allan Poe's 'The purloined letter'), rather than, as for Freud, something to be analysed (his reading of E. T. A. Hoffmann's 'The sandman'). In order to explicate the analytic effect of subjecting oneself to the uncanny I make use of an elegy by William Wordsworth.

A discussion of Lacan's seminar on *Hamlet* enables me to elaborate further what Lacan makes of literary and artistic works in the context of his theory of language and of the constitution of the subject in the dialectic of desire and drive. For Lacan, *Hamlet* is the tragedy of one who has not found the way of his desire and is thus at the mercy of undirected drive. Since the play is all about the subject's flawed entry into the symbolic, a fate common to all, an analytic effect is produced because we are forced to confront the painful engagement of drive with the Other's desire. For Lacan it is Hamlet's refusal to mourn which is central to the dynamics of the play, since absence of mourning, as we have already seen with Kristeva, is an inability to make the sacrifice demanded by the symbolic. Rather than see Hamlet's relation to his mother purely in Oedipal terms, as Freud does, Lacan shifts the focus to the (m)Other's desire as a crucial factor in blocking Hamlet's investiture as a subject of desire. That is why Ophelia ceases to be an object of desire, inertly caught in Hamlet's perverse fantasy, no longer representing life.

The endless effort to become inscribed in the symbolic is the driving force of Robert Coover's *Spanking the Maid* (1982), in which two characters, cast in the role of master and maid, repetitiously perform a ritual of domination and submission. Through its figures, its chronic and playful slippages of language, its rhythms, and the constant struggle of its characters to find words to legitimate their perverse practices, the text performs and enacts the illusory literalness of language in a series of spectacular puns. The text paradoxically demonstrates what the man and woman fail to do in their respectively obsessive and hysterical concentration on a puritan discourse. Their literal attempt to inscribe the Law upon the body re-

sults in an extravagant upholding of the Law and an extravagant stimulation of desire, implicating the reader in an analysis of the perverse.

For Lacan the problematic of femininity is central to the
constitution of the subject. In Krzysztof Kieslowski's film *The
Double Life of Véronique* the question of woman's subjectivity
is intimately explored through posing the question of woman's existence, thereby illustrating Lacan's claim that she is
more subject than man, in that she is aware that her self-
representation is not a mask concealing her 'inner' person, but
a 'masquerade' where her life is lived. The significant differences in the experiences of two women, apparently identical,
are examined by making the voice the central structural feature of the film. In the libidinal economy of the subject the
voice represents an invocatory fantasy, originating in the
(m)Other's voice (at the beginning of the film), from which
point onwards the subject strives to be heard and recognized
by the Other. Whereas in the first case the woman's sexuality
is directed towards the male version of the symbolic, in the
second case the woman demonstrates a capacity not to be
duped by the apparent substantiality of the symbolic, which
spares her the illusion that she is wholly encompassed by it.
The trope of twinship is here used to raise the question of
what a woman wants.

In Part III the focus is on the rhetoric of the clinical session
and the further poetic effects of the transmission of this case
material to others. I first discuss the findings of a forum which
set out to compare different responses to a single clinical case.
The variety of theoretical orientations adopted revealed different commitments, and hence different clinical strategies and
different interpretations were proposed. As a consequence
various therapeutic effects were claimed to be feasible. The
greater the awareness of a range of possible meanings on the
part of the therapist, the greater the choice of what is and is
not to be imparted to the patient. But this raises the problem
of why one choice might be regarded as better than another
and thus in what direction the treatment is to go. Crucially
there is the question of what is to be taken as evidence to
support such a choice when that which is regarded as relevant

is governed by the particular theory being applied. I take up the question of what sort of criteria have to be adduced in order to establish psychoanalysis as a science. Unlike the so-called exact sciences psychoanalysis does not operate with the assumption of an impartial observer faced with a set of countable entities, but inquires into the very construction of the subject/object dichotomy. The analyst is essentially not an impartial observer for she or he is as much subject to the poetics of the clinical discourse as is the analysand.

Whatever the resonance of the analyst's fantasies with those of the patient – the essential factor in unconscious speaking to unconscious, the training of the analyst and her or his own analysis should ensure that this resonance does not contaminate the treatment. Using a Freudo-Lacanian orientation I now discuss extracts from the verbatim analysis, carried out in France, of a psychotic nine-year-old boy, in order to show an analytic couple at work. The analyst, Joyce McDougall, works by identifying the primitive conflicts of her patient while at the same time allowing him to dictate the pace at which he can move through his fantasies without falling into terror. She does this by an astute handling of the poetics of the unconscious in that she enters into the unconscious figures and rhythms her patient produces and reinserts them patiently into narratives of his own devising. Although her orientation as a Freudo-Kleinian is clear, she does not use it to foreclose her patient's thoughts and fantasies, nor does she intrude her own. The analyst pays tribute to her supervisor who co-published the book with her and whose insights she incorporates in her account of the treatment.

I then look at what is more generally involved in clinical management by first considering the rhetoric of supervision as it appears in a series of seminars conducted for analysts by Wilfred Bion, and second by discussing an example of the special kind of family therapy carried out by Salvador Minuchin in the USA. In the example of Bion, the instances he uses to recommend that the analyst challenge the patient's concepts become the rhetorical means whereby he persuades his supervisees to adopt the necessary technique: he conveys to them the patient's self-engrossed picture of the world in a mode that gives them clues to how it can be shaken. He thus shows his supervisees how to enable the patient to digest what she or he would otherwise be prone to reject. In a not dissimilar technique, though through a more dramatic mode of intervention, Minuchin endeavours to develop material implicit in the family's dynamics in a direction more favourable to the autonomy of its members but without entering into open contradiction. He realigns existing loyalties to get a fairer balance of interests, often protecting those whose rhetorical position is weak in the family hierarchy. He manages to elicit from those who are unconsciously colluding with the pathology of the sufferer evidence of their own complicity and uses it to shift their power relations.

Finally I consider the poetic strategies of the writer when she is tempted to engage with an experience that bears all the hallmarks of a clinical case. Elfriede Jelinek's *The Piano Teacher* participates in the 'borderline' pathology of its main character, so that here the clinical and the aesthetic combine in one text, as in the analyst Julia Kristeva's work. In investigating the poetic strategies of the text I reveal a clinical substratum which enriches it, whereby what transpires in the life of the characters repeats itself in the text as a whole. This points to the hazards that equally attend the clinical and aesthetic ventures, since the unconscious is a force that is not easily reckoned with, whether in the case of patients and analysts or readers and texts.

Part I
Psychoanalysis and Literature: Freud

1

What is a psychoanalytic reading?

Psychoanalysis can explain why language is literary all the time, why it is irrepressibly figural. Although Freud always ceded the discovery of the unconscious to the poet, even if at times somewhat anxiously, before psychoanalysis came on the scene, the critic was not conscious of what the literary text might harbour. Deconstruction, for instance, whose practitioners often make themselves independent of psychoanalytic theory, could hardly have got off the ground without a theory of the unconscious. In seeing that meaning was at once always too much and never enough, both supplementary and lacking, deconstruction battened on Freud's repeated linguistic discovery throughout his work, namely, that desire cannot name itself except by substitution.

What, then, is there to be gained from a psychoanalytic reading? Furthermore, a much debated question, what *is* a psychoanalytic reading? I would like to begin with a practical example, a nonsense poem by Edward Lear:

The Owl and the Pussy-Cat

The Owl and the Pussy-Cat went to sea
 In a beautiful pea-green boat.
They took some honey, and plenty of money,
 Wrapped up in a five-pound note.
The Owl looked up to the Stars above
 And sang to a small guitar,

'Oh lovely Pussy! O Pussy, my love,
What a beautiful Pussy you are,
        You are,
        You are!
What a beautiful Pussy you are!'

Pussy said to the Owl, 'You elegant fowl!
 How charmingly sweet you sing!
O let us be married! Too long we have tarried:
 But what shall we do for a ring?'
They sailed away for a year and a day,
 To the land where the Bong-tree grows,
And there in a wood a Piggy-wig stood
 With a ring at the end of his nose,
        His nose,
        His nose,
With a ring at the end of his nose.

'Dear Pig, are you willing to sell for one shilling
 Your ring?' Said the Piggy, 'I will.'
So they took it away, and were married next day
 By the turkey who lives on the hill.
They dined on mince, and slices of quince,
 Which they ate with a runcible spoon;
And hand in hand, on the edge of the sand,
 They danced by the light of the moon,
        The moon,
        The moon,
They danced by the light of the moon.

Going back to Freud's underlying concern with the question
of who had got to the unconscious first, the poet or the psychoanalyst, we might say that the literary critic is here not
sure whether she is an analyst-owl among the analysand-cats,
who have much to learn from her, or, vice versa, whether she
is an analysand-cat, who has much to learn from the analyst-
owls, the clinicians. Or, as some might argue, are the two discourses critically incompatible?

Of course, 'The Owl and the Pussy-Cat' can be enjoyably
read as 'just a nonsense poem'. Composers have chosen to set
it to music for its strong rhythmic qualities, including its rep-

etitions, internal rhymes and refrain. It is also a story because it poses and resolves a problem through a transformation (nose-ring into wedding ring, making two into one), and its setting is a romantic scene – with a courtship, a sea journey, a far-away hill, a song to a guitar, the stars, the moon, a marriage and a celebratory feast. In addition, the poem follows the topos of a fairy tale in having animal characters, one of whom is a helping figure ('said the Piggy, "I will"'). What could psychoanalysis possibly add to this account which might explain the lasting popularity of this apparently naively childlike poem?

Lear's poem might also be read as a bold transgressive fantasy about two creatures from genera with two different reproductive systems (read also 'generations'– the root of both words comes from the Indo-European root *gen*, meaning 'to beget, to generate, produce'). Hence the two creatures require superior assistance, and, because it is a kind of fairy tale, they get it: they take their liquids and their solids – their honey and their money— first to the libidinal pig in the wood and then to the phallic turkey, residing on a hill, in order to gain access to the Bong-tree. For their wedding feast they dine on a hitherto impossible plenitude of food (a menu of mince instead of mice). And finally they couple in that liminal space, the seashore.

The implement the couple use for their feast is a 'runcible spoon'. This is a nonsense term invented by Lear for a three-pronged fork hollowed out like a spoon, which has one prong with a cutting edge: hence it is an object which defies categories, wanting to be fork, knife, and spoon all at once. So it cannot fit into one genus – except in fantasy, like the union of the Owl and the Pussy-Cat. It happens that Lear's nonsense work is particularly characterized by its confusion of categories, both in its writing and its drawing.

Non-sense poetry is a (joking) refusal to accept the boundaries of language. Psychoanalysis has a theory about such a refusal, as will be seen. A psychoanalytic reading might thus take up this confusion of boundaries and read the poem as a set of fundamental fantasies, a denial of castration in its wish to transgress familial boundaries and an attempt to answer a series of questions about the riddles of procreation and sexual difference. But are they Lear's fantasies? There is no way we can know. What the above reading testifies to is the power of the poem to arouse such fantasies in a reader. If such a reading is rhetorically convincing to others, then one could argue that the poem's popularity with readers of all ages testifies to its capacity to provoke primal fantasies, defined as 'typical phantasy structures';[1] these include intra-uterine existence (the sea), seduction (the serenade in the boat), primal scene (the coupling) and (denial of) castration (confusion of categories).

But is it after all nothing but an endearing transgressive fantasy? Some time ago I heard the poem sung as a cabaret item by a hired group at a party where there was a majority of men. The singer, a woman, put a particular emphasis on the refrain, 'what a beautiful *Pussy* you are', thereby alluding to a woman's sexual organs. The *poetic* effect was that of castration, for, first, the woman was alluded to as metaphorically reduced to a cat, and, second, as metonymically further reduced to being merely a part of a cat, since her sexual organs were represented by nothing more than the cat's fur. The 'harmlessly' amusing salacious emphasis unconsciously indicated the horror that lurked beneath the wish-fulfilment.

So what can be said about the nature of a psychoanalytic reading on the basis of this brief discussion? If we set aside the main literary element in 'The Owl and the Pussy-Cat', ignoring the facts that its genre is that of a fable where fantastic elements are normal and that everyone reads it as a nonsense poem, then we can see the uncanniness of two animals, enemies by nature, libidinally incompatible, courting each other. Psychoanalytic theory rests on the assumption that sexuality is the crucial factor in the constitution of the subject. In its clinical practice it relies on finding structural images in the mind, pointing to the way the present is determined by the past in terms of a subject's sexual history. The beginning, the pre-genital, is seen as the loss experienced by the subject upon its separation from the mother's body, the genital being the provisional endpoint, never totally achieved. In Freud's terms sexuality is 'polymorphously perverse', since there is always a nostalgic longing for the infantile variability of sexual satisfaction.[2] A psychoanalytic reading therefore primarily involves being alert to the presence of sexuality in the text. Since we are sexually identified by means of language and since we can be altered by language, we suffer the imprint of the desires of others: every statement is a redirection of someone's desire. Thus the relation of desire and language crucially ties together the psychoanalytic and the literary.

2

The uncanny and its poetics

In order to argue for the measure of Freud's contribution, I would like to examine the Freudian inspiration, particularly in its impact on our understanding of the relation between desire and language, which is later more fully articulated in Lacan's formulations. A good place to begin is Freud's elaboration of the concept of 'the uncanny', a key example of the irrepressibility of the unconscious. Freud's definition of the uncanny is to be found in his celebrated essay of that name.[1] According to Freud, the uncanny is 'undoubtedly related to what is frightening – to what arouses dread and horror'.[2] He defines what characterizes the uncanny by examining the German word for it, *unheimlich*. He writes: '*Unheimlich* is in some way or other a species of *heimlich*', and '*heimlich* is a word the meaning of which develops in the direction of ambivalence.'[3] For *heimlich* means not only homely and familiar, but also hidden and secret. The *un-* of the *unheimlich* marks the return of the repressed material: the word or thing threatens us in some way by no longer fitting the desired context. Hence the uncanny has the effect of destabilizing language. Modern critical theory has moved on from the structuralist perception that words refer to each other rather than to things to the further recognition that this perception ignores the uncanny effect upon language of that to which it seeks to refer.

The uncanny and Surrealism

The concept of the uncanny has become important in postmodern aesthetics because it acts as a challenge to representation. It makes us see the world not as ready-made for description, depiction or portrayal (common terms applied to what an artist or writer does), but as in a constant process of construction, deconstruction and reconstruction. Freud could not understand why the Surrealists were so interested in psychoanalysis. In 1932 he wrote a letter to André Breton, who had accused Freud of not analysing his own dreams sufficiently, and in it he says that he is far from sure what Surrealism is about.[4] Freud felt that one could not analyse the productions of the Surrealists because the analytic process cannot take place in public: psychoanalysis has a theory which gives an account of how and why repressed material suddenly disrupts our familiar ways of perceiving the world, but it sees this theory as grounded in clinical practice. The psychoanalytic process of so-called 'free association' is not to be equated with automatic writing, for instance, because, unlike what the Surrealists hoped, there is no pure truth which can emerge undisguised and uncensored from the unconscious. The freedom of free association is not to be understood as an absence of determination, but rather as overruling the voluntary selection of thoughts. What one overrules thereby is the censorship between the conscious and pre-conscious (that which is not present to consciousness). The unconscious defences reveal themselves in the material that the analysand produces in the course of analysis. This material is not a direct expression of the impulses of drive, but consists of ideas or images that have attached themselves to these impulses, what Freud calls 'ideational representatives'. Consequently, the return of the repressed is not the return of such an impulse but the return of whatever idea or image has attached itself to it. It is only when the analyst and analysand 'work through' – as Freud calls it – the repeated emergence of these images and thoughts that the unconscious fantasy can be pieced together.

The popular account of Surrealism, including Breton's own,

relates it to the dream and argues that the unconscious emerges in a dreamlike manner in the techniques of collage and automatic writing. But Theodor Adorno, in an essay entitled 'Looking back on Surrealism',[5] questions whether we should necessarily accept the Surrealists' own understanding of what they are doing, since this is tantamount to explaining the strange by the familiar, by what we already understand. Adorno argues that, if Surrealism is taken to be no more than a literary and graphic illustration of Freudian or Jungian theory, it becomes just a harmless reduplication of what the theory tells us – hardly the kind of scandal that is the very life-blood of Surrealism; if we view Surrealism simply in terms of Freudian theory, we miss the peculiar power of this movement. According to Adorno, no one dreams in the Surrealist mode: to equate Surrealism with dreaming is at best a crude analogy. The images in Surrealist art split into parts, and then these parts are treated with odd respect, as if they were autonomous forms, wholes in their own right. In Surrealist art, objects are most carefully chosen and placed, in just this space, next to another object just this size. To understand what is going on one has to look at this art's strategies, its use of collage and montage, which enables images – whether in poetry or in painting – to be juxtaposed in patterns of discontinuity. It is this which gives Surrealism its shock value, provoking that sense of 'where have I seen this before?', the *heimlich* (homely and familiar) combined with the *unheimlich* (hidden and secret). Adorno maintains that the affinity of Surrealism and psychoanalysis depends not on their common interest in the symbols utilized by a truth-speaking unconscious, but rather on the way in which they both focus on the images of our childhood, a past crystallized within us. The giant egg, for instance, from which a monster threatens to emerge at any moment, is big because we were so very small when we first gazed at an egg in extreme trepidation. The uncanny effect is brought about because we are confronted with a subjectivity now alien to us, having had to move on. What produces shock, in his view, is that twilight state between a schizophrenic sense of the world split into parts, either chopped up or threatening to merge, and the apparent autonomy and self-sufficiency that these parts assume. The apparent freedom from normal representation becomes threatening, leading to a kind of death, either because objects become rigid and unchanging, or because they melt, flow and dissolve. These images, Adorno argues, are fetishes, objects once invested with emotion but now estranged, left over from the past, dead substitutes for what is no longer.

It is useful, then, to discuss the uncanny effects in the visual arts from the psychoanalytic point of view. René Magritte's pictures of severed breasts, legs in silk stockings, shoes with human toes, the nose, eyes and lips floating in space, are reminders of what Freud calls '*Objekte der Partialtriebe*', later developed by Melanie Klein in her theory of the part-object. These objects of the partial drives (for example, an oral or an anal drive) are sexual drives functioning independently of any overall organization; they can be observed in the fragmented sexual activities of children and also in the sexual life of adults. We are reminded of how libido, the energy of the sexual drives, first started off by attaching itself to whatever the senses perceived as significant at the time, but which now belongs to a history of repression. This is why this kind of object is *unheimlich*: we are seeing our old childhood wishes that we have long since had to repress. The distortions of the object bear witness to the taboos and interdictions we had to observe, and to what these taboos have done to our past desires. But what this ignores, as discussed below, is that the uncanny can also be viewed as subversive rather than merely regressive.

One of Magritte's paintings will serve as an example of the characteristic co-presence of *heimlich* and *unheimlich* elements in Surrealist art. At first sight his *The Art of Living* appears to be like a child's picture of the sun, oddly placed, because the sun is in front of a mountain, hence more important than the mountain behind it. The sun as king-image is suddenly turned into a man or father-image by means of a small face in the middle of its large sphere, with the body underneath dressed in a suit. But the sun also looks like a head that has been severed, as if it were the fearful realization of a repressed wish. At the very moment when this wish is gaining expression, it emerges as a threat, in the fixed stare of the face. The picture thus combines the abnormality of the *unheimlich* with the normality of the *heimlich* – the dress suit and tie on the body against a brick wall at the front of the picture, towered over by the huge and lurid sun. The very title, *The Art of Living* suggests having to come to terms with the repression demanded by the father; the sun is so very big because the father (or the Law) once seemed, and in the unconscious still seems, so very powerful. Surrealism furnishes us, according to Adorno, with an 'album of idiosyncrasies', objects which say 'no' to desire; and, if the object strikes us as obsolete, it is because we do not wish to be reminded of the failures of desire of which it speaks.

This perceptual world which strikes us as obsolete, which we once hallucinated and thought we controlled, whose animistic modes of perception Freud speaks of in 'The uncanny', makes no distinction between self and other, me and not-me. It is the infant's world of primary narcissism, which defies any notions of commonsense reality. Fantasy, Freud tells us, is intimately connected with an archaic mental theory, with the belief in the 'omnipotence of thoughts':

> Our analysis of instances of the uncanny has led us back to the old, animistic conception of the universe. This was characterized by the idea that the world was peopled with the spirits of human beings; by the subject's narcissistic overvaluation of his own mental processes; by the belief in the omnipotence of thoughts and the techniques of magic based on that belief; by the attribution to various outside persons and things of carefully graded magical powers, or '*mana*'; as well as by all the other creations with the help of which man, in the unrestricted narcissism of that stage of development, strove to fend off the manifest prohibitions of reality. It seems as if each one of us had been through a phase of individual development corresponding to this animistic stage in primitive men, that none of us has passed through it without preserving certain residues and traces of it which are still capable of manifesting themselves, and that everything which now strikes us as 'uncanny' fulfils the condition of touching those residues of animistic mental activity within us and bringing them to expression.[6]

This is how Freud summarizes the dual uncanny effect of the unconscious:

> An uncanny experience occurs either when infantile complexes which have been repressed are once more revived by some impression, or when primitive beliefs which have been surmounted seem once more confirmed. Finally, we must not let our predilection for smooth solutions and lucid expression blind us to the fact that these two classes of the uncanny are not always sharply distinguishable. When we consider that primitive beliefs are most intimately connected with infantile complexes, and are, in fact, based on them, we shall not be greatly astonished to find that the distinction is often a hazy one.[7]

The uncanny is a projection of our inner fears onto the external, creating objects of love and hate. Fantasy can remake reality, and the instrument with which it does so is projection. Through projection, fantasy discharges itself into the world, but when the object thus singled out fails us, it is experienced as uncanny. In Hoffmann's story 'The sandman', which is central to Freud's essay as an example of the uncanny, the doll Olympia serves as an ideal mirror-image by means of which the suffering protagonist unsuccessfully tries to reconstruct his shattered self-image. The automaton-doll becomes an uncanny object, standing for all objects, which, similarly, are not able to fulfil our desires for ever. The story is an allegory of the uncanny in life: the favoured object turns into an object of fear just as the beautiful Olympia in the story turned into a rigid automaton which is dismembered before the protagonist's eyes. Automata are uncanny objects precisely because of their rigidity, their determined and inexorable behaviour. The reader of 'The sandman', or anyone who has watched an automaton in fascination, senses something of the fear of being driven by an uncontrollable impulse from within: the object becomes *unheimlich* when the repressed impulse breaks through. The uncanny is the return of the repressed, the feared desire-fantasy, and, according to Freud, its occurrence in art is different from that in life because the artist has his own resources for making it appear or disappear. By virtue of his skill he can create the right context for the emergence of the uncanny, whereas in life one has to wait for the context in which it will emerge – the moment when the symptom appears, or the forgotten name is on the tip of one's tongue, or a joke happens, or the picture-language of the dream is unravelled.

Unsurprisingly, the uncanny appears in the most unexpected places. A number of critics have pointed out that the repressed returns in Freud's own essay. 'Freud', writes Hélène Cixous, 'has hardly anything to envy Hoffmann for his "art and craftiness" in provoking the *unheimlich* effect'.[8] For even as he analyses the uncanny effects in Hoffmann's story, his own text displays similar effects. It is disrupted by repeated images of dismembered bodies, effects of the unconscious which reveal anxiety about death, and anxiety about his own priority as the discoverer of the unconscious – whether it is he or the poets who better understand its uncanny effects.

However, the uncanny need not only be seen in a negative way, as necessarily involving regression. According to more recent readings of the uncanny which redefine the sublime, its indeterminate factor provides the shock which allows us to challenge the old boundaries[9] (see also chapter 5 below). This makes the Freudian reading of the uncanny in his essay unduly pessimistic, for it can be argued that Surrealism contains a strongly subversive element: the disturbance of the structure of our old desires can also be a sign that it is time to think about changing self and world. The French philosopher Jean-François Lyotard describes the field from which the uncanny emerges as 'the unpresentable', meaning that something is happening which eludes representation.[10] The uncanny may thus be seen as a basis for a positive aesthetic, a moment when new possibilities, new meanings, may emerge, rather than as a moment when the old repressed meaning returns.

What is involved for Breton in the moment when the object fails may be termed the failure of the category, and he made this failure a central theme of the Surrealist manifesto. He writes of a 'crust of exclusive signification with which usage coats all words',[11] in which an old system out of touch with present reality tries to trap the individual. Breton wants to shake loose the self – the subject in process rather than the self assumed to be there from the beginning – away from a rigid order which no longer serves either the subject or its society. For it is not only the subject who has got stuck; history and society have also got stuck in repeating the old repression. The emergence of the uncanny may be the moment which disturbs our narcissistic gaze, the moment which allows us to see that the old repression is futile, a waste of energy – 'uneconomic' in both its Freudian and its material sense, serving neither useful psychic nor utilitarian purposes – and that a redirection of desire is called for.

This jolting into awareness is performed in another example from Magritte. His well-known image of a round-bowled pipe with a curved stem provides a comforting picture of a homely object until you see the caption *Ceci n'est pas une pipe* ('This is not a pipe'), which reminds you that it is only a representation, and that appearances are fooling you. The picture is uncanny because it has the further implication that in the actual world you also depend on appearances: the pipe might break, have no tobacco, not light up, fail to give the hoped-for reassurance. Michel Foucault points out that the words themselves represent something which is uncanny: if *ceci*, meaning 'this', is taken to refer to the phrase, the result is that one realizes that words are not pipes, that language has no direct relation to the object which it replaces.[12] Language, instead of being the reliable guide to nature, is shown to fail in its cataloguing of the world. So the picture says both 'this image isn't a pipe', and 'this phrase isn't a pipe', and thus enacts an uncanny invasion of the comforting world where image and language coexist unproblematically.

Freud's 'Wolf Man'

By way of contrast, then, I will now discuss an example from life, taken from the famous case history of the 'Wolf Man'.[13] It was this case which caused Freud to confront the problem of the relation between 'primal scene' (as actual event in which the child observes or infers the parental intercourse) and 'primal fantasy' (as a typical psychic structure of fantasy unconsciously transmitted through the generations). Whatever conclusion Freud finally reached (the structural importance of fantasy as against any real seduction), given that fantasy will be operative in both cases, the patient's account will in either event show the way that fantasy emerges from under a screen of memory. In the course of his treatment of the Wolf Man, Freud gives an account of a scene which serves particularly well to illustrate a moment when repressed material emerges. It shows clearly how fantasy in the psychoanalytic sense has nothing to do with any direct representation of what is desired. The real wish remains hidden. Fantasy is not to be understood in the popular sense of the term, as a wish-fulfilling daydream, but as something the unconscious constructs in order to approach that which is desired and feared.

Freud's patient was a wealthy young Russian who came to have an analysis with him in 1910. In his general survey of the case Freud describes some of the Wolf Man's fears:

> There was a particular picture-book, in which a wolf was represented, standing upright and striding along. Whenever he caught sight of this picture he began to scream like a lunatic that he was afraid of the wolf coming and eating him up. His sister, however, always succeeded in arranging matters so that he was obliged to see this picture, and was delighted at his terror. Meanwhile he was also frightened at other animals as well, big and little. Once he was running after a beautiful big butterfly, with striped yellow wings which ended in points, in the hope of catching it. He was suddenly seized with a terrible fear of the creature, and screaming, gave up the chase. He also felt fear and loathing of beetles and caterpillars. Yet he could also remember that at this very time he used to torment beetles and cut caterpillars to pieces. Horses, too, gave him an uncanny feeling. If a horse was beaten he began to scream, and was once obliged to leave a circus on that account.[14]

It is not the objects in themselves, however, which provoke the fear, but what they represent in the structure of the unconscious fantasy, as can be shown by one of the dreams that the Wolf Man relates to Freud. In this dream a man is tearing off the wings of an 'Espe'. Freud was puzzled by this and asked what he meant. The Wolf Man answered that he meant the insect with the yellow stripes on its body that stings. Since German was not the Wolf Man's native language, his mistake could look like a natural one, *Espe* for *Wespe* (wasp). However, as pronounced in German, the initials of the Wolf Man's name were 'S.P.', hence *Espe*. There are thus two meanings for one sound, an *unheimlich* one (wasp) and a *heimlich* one (the Wolf Man's name), forging a link between the mutilated insect and the patient himself. Further associations followed. From an earlier memory of the patient's, Freud had elicited that yellow stripes were associated with a woman, a nursery maid called Grusha. At first Freud thought that maybe this memory had something to do with a striped dress she might have been wearing, but it was not so. In the Wolf Man's language the sound 'Grusha' was also the name of a particular kind of pear with yellow stripes, which the Wolf Man in childhood had found especially delicious. This in turn enabled him to recall the childhood memory of the big butterfly with yellow stripes and large wings, which he had found frightening. The connection between the insect-butterfly and insect-wasp is thus another associative link, overdetermining the form of the later dream, that is to say, letting one element (the stripes) produce more than one meaning. A fantasy – we still do not know what it is about – can thus be displaced and condensed along such a series to any degree of complexity, depending on the associations of the dreamer. The Wolf Man did not know why he was afraid of these images; the fantasy hid the cause. The sequences eventually led back through a recollection of the nursery maid on her knees, scrubbing the floor, to a scenario of a 'primal scene', which presented a copulation *a tergo*. The whole case was a landmark for Freud, precisely because he had to confront the problem of how far these primal scenes, repressed memories of parental intercourse, were real memories or fantasies. But the point that needs stressing is this: in each case, although the content of the fantasy changes, the structure is the same – something seen or heard is given two meanings, a *heimlich* one and an *unheimlich* one.

Figure 1 should make the structure of the dream clear. First there is a sensory element, something seen or heard. Taking the incidents in order of time, the sound / espə / is *heimlich* as the name of the Wolf Man, *unheimlich* as the name of the wasp; the sound /gruʃə/ is *heimlich* as the name of the maid, *unheimlich* as the name of the pear; the stripes are *heimlich* on the butterfly, *unheimlich* on the pear. Grusha, stripes and 'Espe' each have a manifest *heimlich* meaning which veers into a latent *unheimlich* one, illustrating Freud's point in his essay 'The uncanny' that *heimlich* can mean both 'familiar and homely'

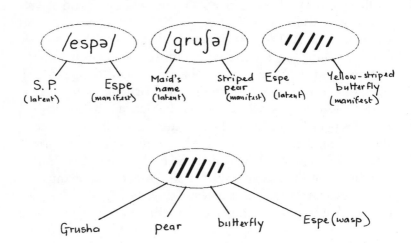

Figure 1   Diagrammatic representation of the Wolf Man's dream.

and 'secret and hidden'. In the Wolf Man's mind all these elements coincide on the yellow stripes. The unconscious made these links without the Wolf Man's conscious knowledge: the fear attached itself to the sensory element, but he does not know why. The real cause is repressed.

Thus, both psychoanalysis and literature partake of the uncanny: a theory of the uncanny is also a theory of literature and the arts. Again we can turn to Freud to ask about the uses of psychoanalysis in the realm of aesthetics. Freud said a great many things about literature and the arts – some of them contradictory – which are beyond the scope of this inquiry.[15] He made two major pronouncements, one to account for the pleasure we derive from our identification with the hero's triumph,[16] and one for what we derive from our identification with the hero's downfall.[17] Although these two pleasures appear to be at opposite poles, what unites them is the capacity of the work of art to offer a disguise and shelter for our narcissism. But how does suffering gratify our narcissism?

There is a social dimension to fantasy in that fantasy can be either shared pleasure or shared suffering: at an unconscious level the suffering itself is enjoyed masochistically. The pleasure of fantasy consoles for the suffering induced by the oppressive symptom, through which the superego exacts payment. This pleasure of fantasy, for Freud, is the imaginary function of art, but he also sees it as having a symbolic function, in that he sees art as achieving a transformation of this narcissism of the id into the narcissism of the ego: the narcissism of the id is the illusion of omnipotence; the narcissism of the ego is the belief that our wishes can coincide perfectly with the social, so that the ego-ideal looks upon us benignly. The transformation is effected when excessive libido is 'desexualized' by being diverted into other channels, a process Freud calls 'sublimation'. The work of art and literature has the capacity to involve both creator and spectator in this process by way of their mutual narcissisms meeting in what has been called by one critic/analyst a 'trans-narcissistic communication'.[18] Through the aesthetic work both artist/writer and spectator/reader momentarily gain freedom, working/playing through the repressed material in an illusion of jointly creating a whole object. This end process, as has been pointed out,[19] is not unlike what Melanie Klein has called 'reparation'.[20] Yet for Freud sublimation is not merely a baptism of the cultural: he also presents sublimation as an operation of the partial, non-genital drives (oral, anal and phallic), thus suggesting the 'perverse' dimension of the social field where libidinal impulses find an outlet in all kinds of substitution.[21]

The upshot of this is that psychoanalysis has shown that the structure of the aesthetic object always produces more or less than the author or reader intends, the object's lure residing in its uncanny power to provoke the reader's unconscious fantasy. Shifts of context outside the reader's control betray the fact that the comfortable reference is no longer what it appeared to be. The uncanny of art and literature blocks the fantasy of narcissistic completion. The psychoanalytic unconscious has substituted the disconcerting notion of the return of the repressed, the uncanny effect *par excellence*, for the humanist critic's notion of a rich plenitude of ambiguity. The Freudian notion of art's function in culture is, nevertheless, ultimately a consoling one. For Freud, art and literature gratify unconscious wishes, even where that wish is a perverse one.

3

The vagaries of fantasy: Alfred Kubin's The Other Side

For Freud 'the motive forces of all phantasies are unsatisfied wishes, and every single fantasy is the fulfilment of a wish, a correction of an unsatisfying reality'.[1] This entails 'work' on the part of the artist to enable the wishful fantasy to reach the light of 'day' in disguise. In his essay 'Creative writers and daydreaming'[2] Freud treats fantasy exclusively in its daydream aspect. Although he alludes to the element of shame that is often associated with personal fantasies, in this essay he does not deal with any underlying unconscious and conflictual fantasies. However, he mentions in passing that, if fantasies become too powerful, they can act as a trigger for neurosis or psychosis: 'here a broad by-path branches off into pathology' (p. 136).

Freud thereby touches on the ambiguous nature of wish-fulfilment, where unconscious fantasy is working within the conscious daydream, a factor which he recognizes in his essay on 'psychopathological drama',[3] in which he discusses how the audience's experience of repressed material might provide a kind of satisfaction remote from that of the daydream. Indeed, the whole of *The Interpretation of Dreams* is about unconscious impulses seeking fulfilment through the indirections of the dream, the code the wish adopts to get past the censor to the light of day. Freud sees dreams, symptoms, jokes and all manner of Freudian slips as derivatives of unconscious fantasy, but recognizes that not all fantasies can become conscious. Fantasies have close links with desire since they get attached to primordial memories of satisfaction, encouraging the hallucinatory return of this satisfaction. Hence the relation between fantasy and desire is complicated because it is not so much an object that is wanted but a scenario which requires the presence of the subject.

To bring out the hazardous nature of fantasy I want to discuss a novel first published in German in 1909, Alfred Kubin's *The Other Side*.[4] Kubin declared that its 'principal meaning' for him was that 'it is not only in the bizarre, exalted or comic moments of our existence that the highest value lies, but that the painful, the indifferent, and the incidental-commonplace contain these same mysteries ... one thing is certain, fantasy has put its hallmark on my existence, it is fantasy that makes me happy and makes me sad'.[5] Kubin, a graphic artist and prolific illustrator, wrote this his only work of fiction in twelve weeks and illustrated it in another four weeks. The central figure of the novel is a thirty-year-old graphic artist from Munich, whose life is suddenly disrupted by an unknown visitor, who brings to him and his wife an invitation from an old schoolfriend that they are to come and live in an unknown country somewhere in deepest Asia. After a long journey the couple arrive at the frontier. There they enter the country through a tunnel, a 'black hole', to find that the founder and Master of the so-called Dream Kingdom, Claus Patera – the old schoolfriend – remains mysteriously inaccessible. He appears to rule his subjects by some kind of magnetic force. Although he is reputed to be opposed to all change, the couple immediately find something strangely familiar in the unfamiliar: 'So this is Perle, the capital of the Dream Kingdom! Why, this is the way it looks in our worst slums!' (p. 51). This *unheimlich* impression is never quite dispelled, aided by the fact that the buildings have been transported piece by piece from ancient Europe. The garments worn by the inhabitants are also oddly out of fashion, with men in frockcoats and women in crinolines: 'the effect was exactly like masquerade' (p. 61).

Newcomers to the Dream Kingdom are carefully screened

before being admitted, yet they are also in some way predestined. Care is taken that whatever their appearance, their acts in the community will not disturb the people's imaginary investments in the dream state. They live only 'in moods', their external communal existence supplying only the 'raw material', while each individual dream is fostered: 'to disturb it would be an unimaginable act of high treason' (pp. 14–15). The unimaginable act of high treason would be to interfere with his fantasy and thus to steal the other's enjoyment. What the text progressively reveals is the extent to which the imagination becomes distorted as the illusion in the fantasy becomes totalized. To the degree that a perfect plenitude is believed to be achievable the greater is the vulnerability to a persecutory anxiety, something that is amply displayed in the text. At first everything in the kingdom is at a standstill, but slowly a process of decomposition begins to take hold. After a time, an antagonist to the dream, Hercules Bell, arrives from America to confront Patera and to open the kingdom to scientific and commercial influence. In a battle of epic proportions the kingdom is destroyed in an apocalyptic mode. The Master (the Pater/Father) undergoes a mystical and mythical death, the antagonist departs, and the narrator survives to tell the tale many years later.

The Other Side resonates with Freud's assertion that dream life takes place on another stage, another scene: 'the scene of action of dreams is different from that of waking ideational life',[6] not only in its wording but also in its features, as a place where spatial, temporal and qualitative boundaries are constantly blurred or eroded:

> The sun *never* shone, *never* were the moon or the stars visible at night. The clouds hung low over the earth in unvarying uniformity. (p. 53)

> Natural greens were nowhere to be seen; all the grass, plants, bushes and trees were dyed a dull olive, a greenish grey. (p. 54)

Hence there is no inclination to live in symbolic time. In not recognizing the cycle of life no one wants to take the care of children upon themselves. Children 'by no means compen-

sated for the nuisance they caused', making demands on time
and money without giving any return: 'Who wanted to put
further strain on his nerves or make a woman look older?' (p.
59)

  Similarly, the monetary system— and money is metaphorically and metonymically a trope for the symbolic – has no
relation to value. The designation 'symbolic' is in fact here
downgraded, 'the whole of economic life was "symbolic"', that
is, considered merely imaginary, contrary to the real world in
which coins, and especially paper money, like words, have
exchange value only while people attribute an illusory intrin-
sic value to them. Money depends for its use on its commerce
in the world, where its value will go up and down according
to people's judgements about the goods for which it is ex-
changed, the referents to which it applies. Not so here:

> Anyone coming to the Dream Kingdom would not notice at
> first the constant fraudulence of business life. [. . .] The whole
> of economic life was 'symbolic'. No one ever knew how much
> he owned. Money was brought to you and then taken away
> again, you handed out and you took in. We were all to some
> extent pickpockets, and I too soon learned the dodges. (p. 65)

Thus there were no calculable wins, 'no bargain could be struck
with the invisible reckoner' (p. 66), no viable negotiations
except at an imaginary level.

  Fantasy, far from fulfilling wishes, here designates the subject's impossible relation to desire. It is fantasy that constructs
desire for the subject, in that it is the purported answer to the
enigmatic question of what the Other wants, for it is here that
the desire of the subject is lodged. The Dream Kingdom's inhabitants are in thrall to the ubiquitous gaze of their founder,
Patera, the Big Other as the symbolic *per se* :

> But no matter how confused things were, one felt a *strong hand*.
> Behind even the most incomprehensible circumstances one
> detected its secret mastery. It was the mysterious force by vir-
> tue of which everything was held together and did not topple
> into the abyss. It was the great fate that watched over us all.
> An immense justice, reaching even into hidden places, it

brought all events back into balance. [. . .] That limitless power, full of dreadful curiosity, an eye that penetrated into every nook and cranny, was omnipresent; nothing escaped it. (p. 65)

But everything is far from being 'held together'. A slow accumulation of an ominous substance gradually reveals itself beneath the complacency of the first-person narrative: the egoic, would-be rational view of the world, which tries to make some kind of sense of it, is constantly threatened by the subjective material, which fills the narrator and his wife with 'deathly anxiety', 'choking anguish', 'a torment, driving me on like an engine' (p. 127). A particular moment when such anxiety erupts is when the narrator's wife is in her death throes at the house of the doctor, and the narrator is about to allow himself to be seduced by the doctor's wife, feeling 'immense dim powers begin to stir within me [. . .] somewhere in the depths', and his drive begins to assert itself: 'like lightning, everything changed and coalesced into a single, unwavering intent' (p. 135). Fantasy, bound as it is to the drive, invades the field of the symbolic from the beginning through a variety of demands upon the body. It initially manifests itself through a strange smell coming from the field of the Other, 'a certain indescribable odour that pervaded the whole Dream Kingdom and clung to everything' (p. 74), an 'indefinable substance that one smelled and finally felt with one's whole body' (p. 91).

A yet further invasion of this kind which interferes with the life of the inhabitants is 'an irresistible sleepiness', with the result that the dream state materializes literally, with everyone lunging into sleep on the spot (p. 179). On waking, they find that 'another world had taken possession':

A big green parrot would be sitting on the window sill; or weasels and squirrels would peer out inquisitively from under beds. (p. 182)

Fleas, earwigs, and lice made life miserable. Every species of these creatures, from the biggest to the tiniest, was subject to the elementary instinct of propagation. Despite the fact that they devoured one another, these four- and six-footed pests increased in an uncanny fashion. (p. 183)

Copulation begins to thrive, everything going to it with a riotous appetite. Suddenly the frustrated life substance of the spell-bound city returns with a vengeance:

> Most terrifying were the snakes. No house was safe from their visit; the reptiles lurked in drawers, clothes closets, coat pockets, water pitchers – everywhere. Moreover, the treacherous creatures were of a terrifying fecundity. If you moved about your room in the dark you would step on their eggs which burst with a terrifying plop. (p. 184)

Then slowly and 'most uncanny of all', a great 'crumbling process' begins, attacking everything:

> Cracks appeared simultaneously in all the walls, wood rotted, iron everywhere turned to rust, glassware grew muddy, cloth disintegrated. [. . .] A sickness of lifeless matter. Mold and mildew invaded the best-kept houses.

> Animal excrement in the streets and dust in the houses could no longer be coped with. (p. 189)

All logical and linguistic distinctions begin to blur further, culminating in the loss of language. Fantasy arises at the point where words are not adequate to what they apply to, no longer refer to what the subject wants, where 'reality' fails to satisfy desire:

> It was no longer possible to distinguish night from day; one could barely find one's way in the uniform gray twilight. Since all the clocks had rusted and stopped, there was no method of measuring time. (p. 213)

> Down the slopes from the French Quarter, like a river of lava, slowly poured a mass of dirt, blood, entrails, and carcasses of beasts and men. In this mixture, iridescent with all the colours of decay, the surviving dreamers waded helplessly. They could only babble now and could not understand one another; they had lost the power of speech. (p. 245)

In vain the narrator invokes the Romantic imaginary, seeing a 'natural' symbolic language in the array of sea plants and shells strewn along the shore, a language that seems to have come away from the fallen world: 'Without any doubt there were secrets here; the wings of many splendid insects, nocturnal moths and beetles, bore many marks that must certainly have been a lost alphabet' (p. 195). Although it is a language to which the narrator lacks the key, the Big Other must surely be conversant with it, perhaps even be concealed within it: 'How great you must be, Patera, I thought. Why does the Lord hide himself so mysteriously even from those who love him?' (p. 195) Soon the desire of the Other begins to reassert itself and the narrator, 'filled with an obscure feeling of compulsion', finds himself inexorably pushed and pulled towards the palace, 'mechanically, like a wooden doll, I marched on, one two, one, two' (cf. the automaton in chapter 2 above), hearing his name called repeatedly, fearing to look round and endlessly chanting in his mind 'Patera, Patera' (p. 200). When he finally comes to 'stare' into 'those lustreless eyes', he is spellbound by their gaze, 'like two empty mirrors reflecting infinity', as if Patera were suspended in 'the zone between-two-deaths', to use Lacan's phrase.[7] Already marked with death although still alive, 'Patera was simply not alive – if the dead could see, that would be their look' (p. 201). With the imminent collapse of the Dream Kingdom, the inhabitants' illusion of a communal symbolic, no longer enshrined in language, is unable to hide the fact of death and the cessation of desire which Patera's plan had endlessly seemed to promise to fulfil.

The drive now comes up against a blank wall; the gaze is not what the fantasy had made it out to be, albeit there is an attempt to sustain the illusion. Patera is now among the living dead, changing from the idealized Other (Freud's ego ideal) to its obverse, the father of *jouissance*, who lives on as the obscene superego, encouraging the subject to invest the symbolic with unbridled drive, inciting it to 'enjoy'. The result is the opposite, the destruction of the symbolic by this obscene superego, contrarily demanding punishment for the drive it has released, let go.

> The city had long since disappeared beneath his feet. He stood there upright, his torso reaching to the clouds; his flesh as if

> made of hills. He seemed filled with rage! [. . .] He was bent
> on destroying everything. He spurted boiling urine at far-off
> mountain huts, and their unsuspecting inhabitants were scalded
> to death in the steam. (p. 255)

The symbolic is now infested with the Thing instead of invested with desire: *das Ding* is a term coined by Lacan to des-
ignate the problem of the mother as primal object, a kind of
pre-object, forever ambiguous because the Thing has, on the
one hand, an alien objective aspect, and, on the other, a subjective absorbing one.[8] There is a monstrous vision of a fusion
between Patera as drivebound himself and Hercules Bell as
champion of benighted reason,

> interlocked into an amorphous mass; the American had grown
> completely into Patera. [. . .] The formless creature possessed
> a protean nature; millions of small, changing faces appeared
> on its outer surface; these talked, sang, and screamed confus-
> edly, and then were reabsorbed. (p. 253)

Here, then, is the impossible union of drive and language, where
there is no way in which one voice can emerge from the fusion of all. It was Kant's impossible dream that behind every
phenomenal entity was the noumenal *Ding-an-Sich* , the meta-
physical support of the linguistic identification. At one point
during the uproar of the city's decline, Kubin's text, with a
satirical allusion to Kant, comments on the madness of endeavouring to compel what is heterogeneous ('the Thing-in-
itself') into the categories of language ('other things'):

> Love of the flesh is simply the will of the Thing-in-Itself to
> force its way into the temporal world. How can you be so
> presumptuous as to compel the Thing-in-Itself? You make no
> distinction between the Thing-in-Itself and other things. (p.
> 234)

This was the hairdresser's view of the saturnalia taking place,
and the hairdresser's reward for uttering this theoretical truth
was to be hanged 'from the sign over his shop' (p. 234).

Language, instead of being a locus for the mediation of one

voice against another, turns into a single subject's fantasy of its full accession of drive, an anarchic conviction that the symbolic guarantees the unalloyed, unrestrained achievement of a blissful union in which the pain of division would be expelled for ever. But what the Other wants is specified in language, which implicates and disguises the different peculiarities embodied in each subject and hence will demand some kind of renunciation. 'Reality' is no more than the experimental outcome of every attempt to achieve some kind of coincidence of desire. The horror that results from ignoring this is such that it induces a continual oscillation between the ideal and its obverse: following the battle with Hercules Bell, there is a reverse transformation of Patera, from the terrible father of *jouissance* (the primal father of Freud's *Totem and Taboo*) to the ego ideal, even though the dream kingdom is finally to be extinguished. The eyes have 'now lost all trace of their uncanniness' but are rather gleaming, kind and all-embracing, the great head having become 'marmoreal, cold, like the statue of some god of the ancient world' (pp. 261 and 263), as if the symbolic were on the point of fulfilling all desire.

Kubin's text provides its own explanation for the compulsion to repeat endlessly this attempt to make the symbolic fill the emptiness that confronts the subject, to drive on with the impossible task of getting language to fit the world:

> They had to wrest their imagined world out of the void, and from this imagined world they had to make a conquest of the void. The void was inflexible and it resisted. Then the power of the imagination begun to hum and whir; forms, sounds, smells, and colours began to take shape in every way— and there was the world. But the void devoured everything that has been created and the world became flat, pallid; life rusted, grew silent, fell apart, and was dead again, was nothing. Then it began all over again. (p. 149)

We can recognize in this the Romantic view of creativity in its broadest aspect. According to Samuel Taylor Coleridge, for example, the imagination, the 'esemplastic power', that which shapes into one, has two levels, the first being 'the prime agent of all human perception', the second being a power that 'dissolves, diffuses, dissipates, in order to recreate [. . .] it is essentially *vital* , even as all objects (*as* objects) are essentially fixed and dead'.[9] There is here the recognition that there is a 'power' which is bent both on forming unities and in revising what is produced (Freud's Eros and Thanatos working dialectically). However, this view assumes that the ability to unify parts of our experience constitutes a kind of divine faculty common to all, leading to the belief that a common harmony can be achieved. It is the belief in the possibility of such an ultimate harmony that results in the 'fixed and dead' objects. On the contrary, the conquest of the void is endless, beginning 'all over again', 'recreating', but not through some pre-given 'prime agent' (Coleridge)[10] or 'demiurge' (Kubin).

Kubin's text plays with a final union between word and world and turns it into an inferno, resulting from the attempt to realize a single totalizing fantasy and treating this fantasy as if it could be the fulfilment of a wish. To wrest the 'imagined world' out of what is formless is to employ the Freudo-Lacanian death drive – paradoxically, to awaken the life that 'rusted, grew silent, fell apart' in an endless search for a satisfaction beyond pleasure:[11] fantasy gropes for the satisfaction of the drive, creating 'realities' as substitutes and succeeding only to the extent that it touches on the desires of others that are similarly afflicted by lack in the Other, the lack of a guarantee that the symbolic will finally deliver the longed-for plenitude.

The text has shown the consequences of an abuse of the symbolic. A breakdown of communication took place owing to the monologic discourse of a Master, such that the dialogic nature of discourse was disregarded. In chapter 5, through Lacan, I show how a certain notion of discourse will reveal the social bond to be both possible and impossible. The social bond is essentially a linguistic one, where language is viewed in its widest semiotic sense, as paradoxical, that is, as poetic in its very structure. Where subjects persist in denying this structure they enter into the world of the melancholic, which requires the poetic to deliver them.

4

Maladies of the soul: the poetics of Julia Kristeva

In his essay, 'Creative writers and daydreaming' Freud touched on the relation between art and mourning, but never developed it as Lacan was to do (see chapter 6 below). Language, for Freud, has preserved the connection between *Spiel* ('play') and the forms of imagination involved in the creative representation of the world: 'It speaks of a "*Lustspiel*" or "*Trauerspiel*" ["comedy" or "tragedy": literally, "pleasure play" or "mourning play"] and describes those who carry out the representation as "*Schauspieler*" [literally "showplayers"].'[1]

The work of Julia Kristeva is particularly concerned with this kind of 'showing', both in the literary text and in the analytic situation. Her work points to the rhythms, semantic shifts, changes of intonation and poetic figures which attend the speech of the melancholic. When words are lost, a dialogic communication can emerge in the analytic discourse by means of such rhetorical elements, alleviating pathological states that arise when the subject is 'unbelieving in language', unable to take upon itself 'the bond of faith' which would connect it to others.[2]

Kristeva is a linguist and practising psychoanalyst who did her training with Lacan. In her own work she has developed Freudian thought in line with her interest in pre-verbal material as it occurs in both the clinical session and the literary text. She has written widely in a mode paradigmatic for combining the poetic and the clinical both as regards her subject matter (writers, artists, patients) and through her style (lyrical, polemical, idiosyncratic). I would like to examine the way in which her writings are a testimony to the uncanny nature of both the clinical and the aesthetic: as soon as a concept is arrived at there is another lurking within. In this the melancholic subject is in principle no different from any other subject. However, the melancholic produces an ostensibly lifeless language which nevertheless betrays the dark force of misdirected energies, unlike the aesthetic text, which works 'knowingly' with duplicitous meanings.

In this chapter I look at two works of Kristeva's that bear out this connection between the poetic and the clinical, each work dealing with the psychic disorders peculiar to contemporary life. In *Black Sun: Depression and Melancholia*, Kristeva provides a discourse of the poetics of depression, and thereby creates a dialectical conversation between art and the clinic. She traces the source of depression to an inability of the depressed subject to detach itself from its primal object, the mother, and shows how this produces a trauma of identification. In *New Maladies of the Soul* [3] she makes the problematics of identification and the consequent disturbances of language her central concern. In both works she focuses alike on literary and clinical phenomena.

Black Sun

Kristeva's title, *Black Sun* , derives from the French nineteenth-century poet Gérard de Nerval, who coined the metaphor – reminiscent of Henry Vaughan's 'deep but dazzling darkness' [4] – that indicates

> an insistence without presence, a light without representation: The Thing is an imagined sun, bright and black at the same time. 'It is a well-known fact that one never sees the sun in a dream, although one is often aware of some far brighter light'.(p. 13) [5]

Melancholic suffering invests both the domain of art and that of the clinic. Depressives are mourning the Thing, 'the real that does not lend itself to signification' (p. 13); this is to say that any kind of knowing is marked with loss, always incomplete. What Kristeva is postulating with the help of Nerval's striking image is a failure of archaic representation of the subject's primal object, the mother, the supposed completion of all representation. The depressed person loses all interest in words and actions, in life itself, substituting 'a life that is unlivable, heavy with daily sorrows, tears held back or shed, a total despair, scorching at times, then wan and empty', seeking either an 'avenging death' or a 'liberating' one, living life as 'a wound of deprivation' (pp. 4–5). In her account of the origin of the subject Kristeva insists that 'before the symbolic can exert its effects, a step towards the rejection of the 'maternal entity' by way of the drives must have been achieved.[6] This attempted expulsion can be looked upon as a kind of *Ur-*negation, through which a first venture in the recognition of an external object is made. Kristeva designates this act as an 'abjection': the force of the drives is directed against what is felt to be repulsive, namely, the mother/Thing's all-enveloping presence as 'a power as securing as it is stifling'.[7]

In his remarkable essay 'Mourning and melancholia', Freud describes the melancholic's 'plaint' as stemming from a real or imagined disappointment with a loved one. Unable or unwilling to become detached from the now broken love relation and to make a new start elsewhere, the melancholic makes an identification with the lost object, obliterating the ego, with the result that, paradoxically, she or he becomes the abandoned object, forsaking and forsaken, now plagued by the superego. Freud evokes this sombre state of affairs with a famous formulation:

> Thus the shadow of the object fell upon the ego, and the latter could henceforth be judged by a special agency, as though it were an object, the forsaken object.[8]

Kristeva develops Freud's shadow metaphor:

> We grieve perhaps even more when we glimpse in our lover the shadow of a long lost former loved one. Depression is the hidden face of Narcissus. (p. 5)

Instead of encountering the brightness of an idealized love, the shadow of the lost Thing is 'cast on the fragile self, hardly dissociated from the other, precisely by the *loss* of that essential other' (p. 5). The depressive is 'a radical, sullen atheist' because she or he refuses to enter into the faith of the symbolic, unable to assume the promise that is never to be fulfilled. The bonds of language no longer initiate a favourable response: instead of working as a 'rewards-system', language provokes an 'anxiety-punishment-pair', a slowing-down of bodily movement that is common to both depression and melancholia (p. 10). The depressed person feels permanently deprived of something that is supremely good, irreplaceable and unrepresentable, something that no erotic object can replace, thereby persisting in a hopeless retreat with the 'unnamed Thing' (p. 13).

Kristeva makes much of Freud's notion of 'the "primary identification" with the "father in individual prehistory"'[9] as a possible way of surmounting the loss. The melancholic/depressive suffers from a failure of primary identification, unable to model herself on a figure that has achieved a separation from the Thing. For Freud this early identification with the father, or with the parents as not distinguished from each other, is the origin of the ego ideal.[10] If this primary identification fails to take place, all secondary identifications will be flawed. Instead of acceding to an endless metonymic deferral of the Thing in language, the depressed person is in thrall to its 'black sun', too bedazzled to break into desiring speech. An all-inclusive mood of sadness then becomes a substitute integrity, functioning as a narcissistic device which enables the sufferer to release the psychic energy displaced by the traumatic experience.

Kristeva sees literary and artistic creation as pointing to a remedy which allows sadness to impress itself upon signs so that the symbol becomes responsive to the experience to which it endeavours to refer. A psychic space is thereby cleared for 'the communicable imprints of an affective reality' (p. 22). The 'imaginary father, father in individual prehistory', called upon to help bring about this symbolic feat, has to be brought into conjunction with the 'oedipal father in symbolic law', thus combining the two faces of fatherhood, the affective meaning of early life and the arbitrary system of language. Both aesthetic creation and religious discourse in its mythical dimension can work as remedies against symbolic disarray. They have a salutary effect, as has been understood throughout history, operating cathartically rather than through cognitive understanding:

> If psychoanalysts think they are more efficacious, notably through strengthening the subject's cognitive possibilities, they also owe it to themselves to enrich their practice by paying greater attention to these sublimatory solutions to our crisis, in order to be lucid counterdepressants rather than neutralizing antidepressants. (pp. 24–5)

These solutions can be productive because the depression itself takes a poetic form. Kristeva provides some clinical examples, one of which is the case of 'Helen', a patient given to near-complete inertia, who withdraws to her room in a wordless and thoughtless state, "'as if I were dead but I do not even think of killing myself, nor do I desire to do so, it is as if it had already been done'". In fact she behaves as if she were already dead, *'playing* dead', using death as an image of disintegration and self-effacement (p. 72). Not only does she play dead herself, but her dreams contain images of herself killing children. What horrifies her is their being separate from herself: the faces of these children are those of the disabled child that she once was and that she wants to blot out. It seems to Helen that she is not killing an external frustrating figure but rather the abandoned child with whom she unconsciously identifies, thus making the killing into an act of imaginary suicide. This drama of poetic transformation in which the patient herself creates the actors makes up one form of her depression.

Another characteristic form of depression is what Kristeva calls 'melancholy cannibalism' (p. 12). The refusal to accept loss is here imaged as both a devouring and a containing; it is an attempt to absorb that which is alien and different so as to make its energies one's own. Paradoxically, this is evidence of the pain of losing the other and a sign that the despairing self

is still reaching out. As an example of the melancholy canni-
balistic imagination Kristeva cites one of Helen's dreams, where
she participates in her mother's wedding feast by rending apart
and devouring the wedding guests piecemeal, including her
mother. This aggressiveness was a way of retaining the mother
who was about to abandon her for a man. Because of the feeling of containing the maternal Thing she became fearful of
having an operation: it seemed to her that someone indispen-
sable within her, a constant companion, would be taken away.

In whatever symptomatic form the patient's suffering appears, a poetic transformation is involved. Helen had a period
of promiscuity followed by one of frigidity, both of which were
an expression of omnipotence: the first ostensibly proved that
she had everything, as if there were no boundary because inner and outer were fused; the second asserted that she needed
nothing because 'I have her within me', as if there were no
boundary because there was nothing outside. Helen described
the first period as one of 'erotic feasts', a devouring of the
external, whereas in the second period the frigidity takes the
form of an unresponsive vagina, as if to say 'I am impenetra-
ble, my vagina is dead' (p. 77). With the maternal figure safely
possessed within, an anal retention, she has no call for the
other. In every case where there is substitution for what the
drive is in pursuit of there is transformation, ambiguity, poeisis.

Kristeva insists that the act of mourning poses particular
difficulties for a woman because she has to replace the love
for a woman with that for a man. It requires a 'tremendous
psychic, intellectual, and affective effort [. . .] to find the other
sex as erotic object' (p. 30). She calls having to give up the
mother 'matricide' – a guarantee of individuation, but there
has to be a compensatory substitution for surrendering the
mother as erotic object, a sublimation through social bonds
and creative activity of every kind. If this matricide is not ac-
complished, the maternal Thing, nurtured within, becomes a
parasite, producing a melancholy atrophy of the self. Such an
internalization of the mother leads to the matricidal impulse
being turned upon the self in order to protect and keep her,
which then produces 'an implosive mood that walls itself in
and kills me secretly, very slowly, through permanent bitter-

ness, bouts of sadness or even lethal sleeping pills' (p. 29). All these are symptoms of depressive illness.

In the works of Marguerite Duras the malady of grief derives from a 'malady of death' (p. 221).[11] The characters in her novels are not mere depressives immersed in a personal mourning but are suffering from the effects of major historical catastrophes. After Auschwitz and Hiroshima the twentieth century appears to Duras to harbour 'a passion for death', detectable on many levels, military, economic, social and environmental, leading to a crisis of representation and an invisible disaster of increasing mental disorder. It is almost as if silence is the only appropriate response to the 'nothing' that confronts us. Even so, modern rhetoric finds a voice in this very melancholia through the attempt to keep faith with the memory of the horror by avoiding the popular and the spectacular, often seeking refuge in plainness to the point of apparent banality.

Duras' style is an example of such an 'aesthetics of awkwardness', where 'the truth of pain' holds in check 'the rhetorical celebration, warping it, making it grate, strain and limp' (p. 225). In the films of Duras a similar but milder effect is produced through enigmatic montage, unrecognizable sounds and fragmented speech. Because her books provide neither a point of observation nor any kind of analysis they 'bring us to the verge of madness', rendering it as a threatening immediacy, as 'madness in full daylight' (pp. 227–8). In *La Douleur,* which searingly depicts the slow recovery of life by a barely surviving Dachau victim, the meticulous medical detail of his corporeal struggle combined with the occasional bleak image constitutes the very style itself:

> Life was yet in him, hardly a splinter, but a splinter just the same. Death would launch an attack – a temperature of 103 the first day. Then 104. Then 106. Death was out of breath – 106; the heart quivered like a violin string. Still 106, but it quivers. The heart, we thought, the heart is going to stop. Still 106. Death strikes, as with a battering ram, but the heart is deaf. It isn't possible, the heart is going to stop. (p. 237)[12]

In these blank numbers the very rhythms, signs and forms of sadness make themselves felt as the drive basis of the sym-

bolic. Inscribed in such rhythms are the energies of the 'semiotic', Kristeva's term for the flows in constant motion which
exist within the body before a subject is constituted and which
inevitably become articulated within the structures and forms
of the symbolic. It is the literary combination of semiotic force
and symbolic precision that communicates the affective reality to the reader.

   In the chapter entitled 'Dostoeyevsky: The writing of suffering, and forgiveness', Kristeva writes in praise of suffering.
She develops Freud's classical essay on Dostoevsky,[13] in which
he attributes Dostoevsky's neurotic self-punitiveness to his
paradoxical hatred of and identification with his father (murdered when Dostoevsky was seventeen) as manifested in his
epileptic fits, a symptom of a death wish.[14] Kristeva, though
accepting Freud's etiology of Dostoevsky's melancholy in the
relation to the father, moves away from Freud's preoccupa-
tion with the cause towards the effects perceptible in the artistic outcome. Like Freud, Kristeva begins with the notion of
a primary masochism, which she finds not so much in the
child's relation to the father but rather in the moment of its
separation from the mother, attended by a suffering which is
'the primordial psychic inscription of a break'. She maintains
that both Dostoevsky's life and work bear witness to this 'pre-
cocious, primary affect', to the extent that a melancholy sadness becomes an all-pervading mood in author and character
alike. The drive, instead of emerging as an erotic one seeking
attachment to an object, finds expression in a passionate sadness, 'a hysterical affect', a symptom betraying 'the rebellious
flesh which delights in not submitting to the Word' (pp. 176–
7). These affects interfere with and accompany verbalization,
producing the effect of individual style; they thereby poetically exhibit the unconscious, the emotion as the 'lining' of
the surface coat of words.

   In Kristeva's reading, Dostoevsky believes that being human
is not so much to do with the pursuit of pleasure or gain but
with 'a longing for a voluptuous suffering' (p. 179) which, unlike rage or hate, cannot be directed outwards, but works within,
constantly returning to its ontological source, the primordial
separation. It gains its voluptuous force from a sadism turned

back onto itself, stemming from the inescapable guilt of becoming a subject who cannot fit the Law that brought it into being. It is this guilt which channels the Freudian death drive seeking release from the tension that any boundary creates. Suffering is so immediately ontological because it is itself a proof of the subject's freedom, the pain of choice. Dostoevsky admired the Book of Job precisely because it presented the subject as a transgressor, irremediably at odds with the divine law, yet refusing to disobey God's law. Among his major protagonists are those who endeavour to deny suffering through setting up manic defences against it by negating paternity/divinity altogether. They assume the mantle of the Father/God themselves, their narcissism leading to a rigid self-idealization, as in the notable example of Raskolnikov in *Crime and Punishment*.

What aesthetic device might offer a way out of this dilemma for both writer and character, not to speak of reader? Kristeva proposes forgiveness as both ethical and aesthetic resolution, as a trope that produces a transformation: in analysis, the analyst's 'tact' resides in his ability 'to get in touch with the other through syllables, fragments, and their reconstruction' (p. 189) in order to enable the patient to re-inhabit the speech that their melancholia has devitalized, restoring their pain of choice. The narrative impulse of the novels springs from the resistance of characters such as Raskolnikov to acknowledging the inevitable mismatch between the subject and the law, the flesh and the word, their story being the ultimate recognition in forgiveness of this aporia. This ethical resolution constitutes the poetics of Dostoevsky's work. Through the love of a woman, Raskolnikov finally comes to forgive himself, recognizing that, through murdering his victim, he had virtually murdered himself. In Kristeva's view, whoever partakes of forgiveness, either forgiving or being forgiven, identifies with the imaginary father, benevolent as distinct from tyrannical, thereby arriving at a new enunciation of the symbolic. Forgiveness offers the subject the opportunity to reinscribe itself, to reinvest itself with love and thus re-create that 'dark, unconscious timelessness' in which it can accede to a better lawfulness in which both self and other can renew the bonds of love. All forgiveness has an aesthetic structure, in that it is a transformation of the originary moment common to every subject, a poeisis.

New Maladies of the Soul

In *New Maladies of the Soul* Kristeva follows up the themes of *Black Sun* by conducting a more general investigation into the project of psychoanalysis and the psychic turmoil produced by modern life. She sees psychoanalysis as crossing the boundary between body and soul, taking 'soul' in the sense used by the Latin Stoics and the early Christians when they made a distinction between maladies of the body and those of the soul. She points out that throughout history there were attempts to establish a connection, which in the course of the Enlightenment turned into the view that mental illness was a sign of a sick body. Freud himself remained committed to dualism, theorizing with the concept of drives on the one hand and a 'psychic apparatus' on the other. This resulted in psychoanalysis finding itself forever crossing boundaries between body and soul, soma and psyche, since language simultaneously involves both action and thought, and since it is language which is at the centre of the analytic cure. Although analyst and analysand are both using the same language, their speech nevertheless has to work on a different set of experiences, psychic realities that are not readily reducible to biological causes alone, with the result that each comes to a different (mis)understanding. So where is this psychic reality to be found? Kristeva argues that, while neither cognitive science nor psychoanalysis has yet produced an answer, psychoanalysis at least preoccupies itself with how a soul is made at the interface between mental experience and the concepts that try to manage it. At the present time, however, soul-making is beset by peculiar difficulties stemming from a general communal breakdown. Lacking the social matrix, people have lost access to psychic life to the extent that whatever is pursued provides only an empty narcissistic satisfaction. This results in misrecognized psychosomatic symptoms arising from a language that has lost its libidinal investments. Only through a renewal of language can psychic representation be revived, the lifeless speech of the melancholic and be revitalized by means of a new grammar and rhetoric that current society is patently not providing.

In the chapter entitled 'In times like these, who needs psychoanalysis?' she questions the wisdom of adapting people to a society which is itself maladaptive. The analyst should rather be concerned to discover what kind of indirect protest is represented by the new disorders of the mind, loosely classified as 'borderline', in that they partake of some of the criteria of both neurosis and psychosis.[15] The 'new maladies' go beyond traditional classification in that a narcissistic withdrawal forestalls the establishment of a transference.

> These patients often resemble 'traditional' analysands, but 'maladies of the soul' soon break through their hysteria and obsessional allure – 'maladies of the soul' that are not necessarily psychoses, but that evoke the psychotic patient's inability to symbolize his unbearable traumas. (p. 9)

Borderline conditions are hard to treat because they are frequently accompanied by a deadening of discourse, a retreat from meaning that can be attributed to a denial of its dialogic character. The energy of the drive expends itself in suffering and is thus deflected away from speech: 'a deficiency of psychic representation hinders sensory, sexual, and intellectual life' (p. 9).

As an example of dead language Kristeva cites the case of 'Didier', whose mode of speech was a determined refusal of dialogue. Functioning like an 'invisible Walkman' he would talk incessantly about his life in an expressionless monotone, designed to keep the analyst at bay. When she did manage to punctuate his speech, he adamantly took her words as his own, thus ignoring the dialogic property of speech. The source of his trauma lay in his relationship to his mother who made him her mirror-object, transforming him into a little girl and thus maintaining him in a pre-oedipal identification. As a result he was locked into an 'autoerotic omnipotence' (p. 14), which enfeebled his entry into the symbolic to the extent that he was at the mercy of his drives, unable to find linguistic access to them or to the other. It was only through his paintings that the analyst was able to help him gain access to his fantasies.

In a parallel case a girl was treated by her mother as a boy, even to the extent that her name, 'Martine', was interchangeable with 'Martin'. The mother wanted a boy to be named after the father, who had died during the pregnancy, and hence Martine's sexual identity became erased. As in Didier's case, the patient's language was devitalized, here as an effect of the mother's inconsolable mourning. Consequently there was a split between language and drive which often tempted the patient to treat the session as a scene of intellectual debate and inhibited her attempts at free association. Nevertheless, there was poetic evidence of her trauma in somatic symptoms, such as eczema at the orifices of her body, and rectal bleeding, a protest at the mother's invasion of her body with enemas in childhood. She was also obsessively concerned with borders and entrances, anxiously preoccupied with the security codes that governed them. In contrast to this mute poetics of the unconscious the patient presented few dreams and no fantasies, which indicated a division within her of thought and emotion.

Both these cases were about disturbances of language rooted in traumas of identification. In the chapter 'Joyce the "Gracehoper" or Orpheus's return',[16] Kristeva explores identification as the key theme of James Joyce's *Ulysses*. Joyce's profusion and confusion of verbal representations have long challenged literary critics. They would rather not see this as symptomatic of an insecurity in language, as if Joyce were dismembering the symbolic in an attempt to reach his fantasies, a kind of blasphemous act. According to Kristeva, far from succumbing to the symptom, Joyce analysed it. Hence, although his writing is not itself a symptom, it occupies itself with what is written within the subject, the subject's identifications. Literature has always concerned itself with the vicissitudes of identification – its uncanny metamorphoses and its ambiguous effects on the reader – but Joyce makes the process of identification central to his work.

Kristeva asks what themes and narrative techniques support this view. Identification is a process that takes place between the body and the psychic apparatus (the conceptualizing system), triangulated by an external Other that bestows the symbolic. From the symbolic I gain the very idea of my own singularity and of the plurality of others. The impulse within this process is love, both that which is *eros* (eagerness to incorporate and fuse) and that which is *agape* (unsought, unforced affection). The problem is poetically mapped in the Catholic relation of God the Father and God the Son in the Eucharist, to which Joyce ('the Gracehoper') with his Catholic inheritance was drawn in the ritual of identification with God's body through the eating of the host. The trauma in his own life (his father's failure and his mother's death) led him repeatedly to confront the precariousness of his identity. The notion of transubstantiation – is the host the body of Christ or only a symbol thereof? – recurs throughout his writings, together with the controversies around the consubstantiality of God the Father and God the Son, linked in *Ulysses* with Shakespeare's father and son and his play *Hamlet*. Leopold Bloom's orality (his love of eating kidneys and other offal) is another emergence of this identificatory mechanism which takes the form of *eros*, whereas for Stephen Dedalus the incorporation of knowledge takes that of the sublimated love, *agape*. Kristeva sees these two kinds of love working within the identificatory process as the prototypes of analytic and artistic practice. That is to say, in analysis, the analytic subject brings its *eros* and the analyst responds with *agape*, a trans-narcissistic negotiation that in the aesthetic field implicates the reader/spectator, the writer/artist and the work of art.[17]

When we confront a literary text, our vigilance is undermined, and what is normally repressed unexpectedly returns, despite the narrative forms and processes that seek to contain it – which in themselves can be regarded as symptoms. Unlike many other writers (Kristeva cites Stéphane Mallarmé), Joyce was (unconsciously) aware of this return of the repressed, for he foregrounds the operations of rhetorical forms that are concealed in everyday living, turning 'the symptom upside down' (p. 175), depriving it of its subversive potential. How then can we keep the identificatory process in a healthy state when modern life so threatens it? Kristeva proposes the twin remedies of love and literature, in that both function to keep the process optimally stable in order to allow for a degree of psychic mobility. This can come about only if language is allowed to be permeated by 'pre- or transverbal representations' (p. 175), that is to say, if sensory and affective phenomena are given due place in the determination of meaning – as startlingly exhibited in the carnivalesque modes of *Ulysses*. If this is true, Kristeva asks, would this mean that Joyce is teetering on the edge of psychosis, to the point of identifying with the lawless 'archaic mother' or with an implied author posing as an indifferent god?[18]

Kristeva argues that a better way to understand Joyce's writing is to contrast him with Orpheus. Where Orpheus failed, Joyce succeeds: where Orpheus refused to bow to the symbolic edict (turning away from the darkness of Hades ahead to look back at Eurydice), Dedalus-Bloom not only survives his hell but is also able to gaze at his Molly-Eurydice (in particular in the final monologue). Thus via a transubstantiation he appropriates her text-body, which enables the reader to think and feel as a woman through the gaze of a male narrator, and thereby paradoxically to identify with the complexity of male sexuality.

The term 'identification' is centrally important in analytic theory and practice because identification proceeds by attempting to incorporate external models that can never be wholly assimilated: from the point of view of the symbolic the identification is precise, but from the point of view of the real it is inadequate. Identification is more a matter of empathy than the copying of a pre-existing model. According to Kristeva, the 'economy of writing in general', and particularly in Joyce's case, moves away from the Oedipus complex to 'another intrapsychic experience, before and beyond Oedipus' (p. 177) – the semiotic as the stuff of the symbolic. It is a procedure whereby the attempted absorption of 'I' into Other is complicated by the interactions of symbolic, imaginary and real: on the one hand, the endeavour to inhabit the symbolic is resisted by the real; on the other, the imaginary tries to efface the resultant split through some form of idealization. As Kristeva repeatedly maintains, the primary identification is rooted in the imaginary father, who appears to benignly possess the sexual features of both parents (unlike the phallic mother). In modern analytic treatment the so-called 'borderline' patient requires the analyst to proffer this benevolent primary identification. The ineffectual repression found in these patients (and Kristeva suggests, also in artists today) shows itself both in their words and actions, and has a parallel effect on the analyst, who will need to respond empathetically. The (new) subject cannot come into being without some form of primary identification. This entails a poetic transformation of the patient's self-image through the drive in the other that encourages a corresponding drive in the patient. Kristeva links the idea of Christian *agape* (dispassionate love) with the imaginary father as the object of the mother's love, a 'third party' who represents the final promise of all symbolic struggle. Thus anyone who identifies with him is a 'Gracehoper'. Notable in Joyce's *Ulysses* is the theme of filial *agape* as evidenced in the characters of Leopold Bloom and Stephen Dedalus, and Shakespeare and Hamlet as they make their appearance in the novel.

Identification never succeeds in defining the subject as 'one'. Psychic experience is thus a series of failed identifications, each attempt endlessly replaced by another. In trying so hard we are always on the brink of narcissism, perversion and alienation. In the borderline patient the drive representatives dominate over verbal representations, for she or he is at the mercy of narcissistic and projective identification, where parts of the subject are split off and lodged in another. But this is the case with all identification since it is essentially a continuing, unstable process, subject to an economy that must allow the drive to shift the word ambiguously along. With the artist the identificatory symptom is discharged into style: he is neither under the sway of fixed identification like the believer, nor the bearer of somatic symptoms like the hysteric, but keeps identifications continually in play. They speak in his work, the guiding impulse being not a submission to the mother's desire that he become her phallus, but a creative performance of the role of the imaginary father, that 'ghostly third party' towards whom the mother strives as for a benign benediction – a god as *agape* (p. 180).

Joyce's own uneasy relationship with his parents (father as failed ideal, mother whose abandonment by her son may have advanced her death by cancer) informs the book, colouring its reflections upon identification. In his discussion of *Hamlet*, Stephen Dedalus takes up the question of Shakespeare's concern with the deaths of his own father and son while he was writing the play, which makes for multiple parent-child analogies: God the Father/Christ, John Shakespeare/Shakespeare, Shakespeare/his son Hamnet, the Ghost/Hamlet, Mr Dedalus/Stephen, Bloom as surrogate father/Stephen, Joyce's parents/Joyce, author/text, text/reader. For each of them the themes of death and resurrection serve as metaphors for the splendours and miseries of identification: there is the death of the superegoic father and the resurrection of the father as ego ideal. Kristeva instances a scene in *Ulysses* where Stephen and Bloom are looking in a mirror and seeing Shakespeare's beardless face 'rigid in facial paralysis' (p. 186), figuring on the one hand an impotent dead father and on the other an idealized copiously productive one. The Eucharist has a similar ambivalence, as an ideal to be welcomed in assimilation and as a body to be aggressively devoured. Likewise, Stephen's dazzling monologue on *Hamlet* pursues the parallels between Shakespeare as author, as actor of the Ghost opposite Richard Burbage's Hamlet, as one who has lost his own father and son, and as one who has the text of the play as surrogate son. To be viable, identification with the father has to be effected through a 'heterogeneous transference', combining being and language in a productive uncertainty, requiring a breaking-away from loving the mother and from the loving mother – a juncture from which the maladies of the soul arise but which is also 'the matrix of my eroticism' (p. 184), the impetus towards the forging of the social bond.

Literary creation therefore partakes of both *agape* and *eros*, 'the paternal, symbolic variety and the maternal, drive-related one' (p. 185). Kristeva's criticism, combining as it does the poetic and the clinical, does not shy away from identifying the psyche of the writer with the life of his characters, a distinction which is often falsely upheld, as if only by maintaining this distinction the writer were to be given his full due. To the contrary, she recognizes that the artist's work forms a continuity with his life:

> That *Ulysses* concludes with Molly's monologue is the best example of such a transfusion, which is at once passionate (through the identification and replication of the beloved woman) and symbolic (through the assimilation of her speech). This transfusion characterizes the evolution of all literary characters, and it calls to mind Flaubert's '*Madame Bovary, c'est moi.*' (p. 185)

Joyce's fantasy narcissistically appropriates the plenitude of maternal passion and power while at the same time finding words for it through the sublimatory paternal identification, thereby greedily making use of both his parents. Nevertheless, Joyce himself paid scant heed to the Oedipus complex, being more interested in the kinds of identification with which psychoanalysis is currently preoccupied and which lead to narcissistic and psychotic states. Kristeva suggests that an 'Orpheus complex' (bypassing Oedipus) was Joyce's route to sublimation, for he challenged Apollo-Shakespeare and absorbed Eurydice-Molly, dissolving male and female in a protean style.

For Freud, malady was of the essence of the psyche, because he saw psychic life in an interminable state of construction and destruction. The artist cannot help but reveal this 'malady' in the style and content of the work, inviting the spectator/reader to detect the protest implicit in it: these discontents of civilization are not simply attributable to the pathologies of the individual subjects, many of whom 'in times like these' suffer from narcissistic withdrawal and decline of desire. It is such pathologies that crucially attend upon those who evade the dialogic nature of discourse. The psychoanalytic approach to depression and perversion, as well as to other 'modern' symptoms, shows both the analytic enterprise and the artistic one as reaching out to the very boundaries that offer it the most resistance.

Part II

Psychoanalysis and Language: Lacan

5

What is a discourse?

Discourse is what enables the mediation of 'reality' to take place. One might say that within it each utterance is a proposal, a 'proposition' for shuffling the boundaries of the symbolic. Discourse consists of the attempt by one subject to alter or maintain the desires of another. It is therefore a transindividual and dialogic process, and not the mere transference of meaning from the mind of one subject to another. This misconception found support in structural linguistics, whose originator was Ferdinand de Saussure: if meanings can be unproblematically transferred from one mind to another, this presupposes that words have single meanings that all understand in the same way. Any theory that starts with such a premise has to provide an explanation of how this common meaning is established. Saussure believed that he had a systematic explanation for the identity of word and meaning. His move was to see the verbal sign as an indissoluble bond between sound and meaning, arising out of a historically established order of distinctions in both (such as between 'pin' and 'bin'). His terms for the sound image and the concept were 'signifier' and 'signified': the signifier is one element of a sign in a structured system (*la langue*) , operating by its difference from other features in the system of sounds; the signified is the other element, the concept, similarly placed in an order of thought. This is a negative definition in that difference is installed by a process of negation – this, not that. For Saussure, once these distinctions have been agreed upon, the transference of meaning can take place unproblematically, firmly bonded together, to use his own image, like the two sides of a piece of paper.[1] He did recognize that meanings changed, for he had a notion of *la parole*, that of language in use as distinct from the ideal system of *la langue*, but there was nothing in his theory that could explain how change came about since he ignored experience, the source of meaning.

But language cannot function as what we think of as 'normal' communication with meanings supposedly the same for everyone, as, for instance, in Roman Jakobson's linguistic model.[2] In this model an addresser sends a message to an addressee; the message makes use of a code, normally a language familiar to both parties; the message has a context, a referent; and it is transmitted through a contact, speech or writing. Language is here taken as a transparent medium of communication *through* which the message is sent, and the subject, addresser as well as addressee, is presumed to be 'there', prior to that language and in command of her or his intentions. It is a model that has been variously adopted by schools of criticism. Each element in turn has been at the centre of literary theory. The Romantic critic focuses on the author as addresser, the phenomenological critic on the reader as addressee, the formalist critic on the message as code, the Marxist critic on the context as history and society. Although with the advent of modern literary theory the emphasis has gradually moved from speech to writing as a medium which more readily reveals the interaction of all these elements, any notion of an unconscious undermining the so-called communication process is left out of this model, which assumes that it deals with stable terms and stable positions.

However, language alters that to which it refers because human desires determine what the signified, selected by the signifier, is taken to be. If human desires change, then what is selected as an entity or property from the field of reference will change: language never arrives at truth but at viabilities, one after another. If there were 'real' truths, language would cancel itself out, since, if it were to match the world, there would be no point in speaking. Lacan takes from Saussure the notion of language as a system of signs determined by their difference from each other, but for him the signifier produces a signified through a direct appeal to the field of experience, a positive condition. For Lacan signifier and signified, far from constituting the unity of a sign through the bonding of sound and concept, as they were for Saussure, represent a node of contestation and struggle. Speaking desires can be dangerous: the only way of being in language is to be at odds with it, although language lures us in through the subject's narcissistic hope that the rules will be hers or his.

Lacan's concept of the unconscious is initially a structural one ('the unconscious is structured like a language'), but he moves beyond the tenets of structuralism and poststructuralism. An acknowledgement of structure has to be balanced against a theoretical explanation of its continual adjustment, not to say its failure, its uncanniness, and this is precisely what Lacan does. Language trades on an illusory literalness which is the source of its concealed figurality; the aesthetic recognizes the figural right away – playfully shows the danger of being too literal. Hence it cannot be the case that a metaphorical language opposes an exclusively literal language, the reason being that desire can never reach its object. How then does Lacan conceptualize the relation between desire and language? Unlike Saussure he sees the signifier intervening in the field of experience from which the signified is selected, not as arbitrarily bonded with an already existing signified, as Saussure claimed. Lacan calls this unrepresentable ground 'the real', one of the three orders with which he conceptualizes the psyche. By the real he does not mean mundane reality. The real is the body as part of an undifferentiated nature. For the incipient subject the part of the real that is significant is the mother's body, called '*Das Ding*' by Lacan, and thus 'the impossible', because the real cannot finally be symbolized. It turns up in a subject's relation to desire, making its appearance because our signifying systems cannot be taken literally, cannot exhaust the real: the desired object is never the one we want. What we desire is the primordial lost object, the Thing. It figures in unconscious fantasy as a missing part of the body, a remainder and reminder of the traumatic separation from the mother's body and the body of nature.

Lacan calls this remainder the *objet a*. It is a difficult concept but it is important to grasp it both for Lacan's theory of
language and for the unprecedented function he assigns to
literature and the arts (as discussed below). There is a dialectic involved with the *objet a* that does not simply make it into
an object of desire. In the first place, it is felt as a lack in being,
and hence Lacan calls it the object *cause* of desire; in the second place, it is a fantasy object pursued in the hope of filling
this lack.

The subject constantly searches for its object in every representation as a hoped-for completion of a unity that never
was. The never-satiated desire for unity finds illusory satisfaction in the realm that Lacan calls 'the imaginary', the second
of his three orders. A narcissistic illusion is inaugurated in the
imaginary when the infant takes its image – from a mirror or
through some other impression – to be an ideal ego, posses-
sing the co-ordination and control it has not yet achieved. This
is what Lacan calls the 'mirror stage'.[3] The integral other in
the mirror is me. The imaginary is a way of denying there is
lack: in the imaginary the infant believes that it can be all that
the mother desires. Its attempt is doomed to failure because
its desire is to be what the (m)Other desires, and the mother's
desires are elsewhere, preoccupied with her own lack.

Thus for Lacan desire is always the desire of the Other. This
implies a fundamental alienation of the subject in that it involves the necessary separation from the mother and the introduction of difference. Difference is introduced through the
intervention of the defining Law. In Lacan's version of the
Oedipus, the 'Name-of-the-Father' (in French there is a homo-
phonic pun: *nom* and *non*, 'name' and 'no') functions as a
metaphor for the Law of language, which, as discussed above,
is a differential system. The imaginary phallus – the penis or
plenitude the mother never had, since she is herself subject to
the desire of the Other – is replaced by the symbolic phallus
as a mark of lack for both sexes. In the real the woman does
not lack the phallus, nor is the phallus/penis a never-failing
source of power and fecundity. Hence the Lacanian notion of
mourning for the phallus affects both sexes.

To have a place as a subject among subjects is to accept the divisions of language, to be subjected to a symbol system which is always already there. The price for a place in the symbolic, the last of Lacan's three orders, is the repression of desire, this being the effect of the paternal interdiction, the Father's name/no. When language gives the subject the ability to count itself as different, to count up to two, one might say, the subject has to give up the imaginary union with the mother's body. But, paradoxically, at the very moment when it speaks to another, becomes 'I', 'you', 'she' – it has to 'sacrifice' itself, it 'fades'. This is what Lacan calls the effacement of the subject behind the signifier, since the signifier, as we have seen, can never cover the real of the subject's being. As a consequence the subject clings for consistency to its phantasmatic object of desire, in the hope that it can supplement its loss of being. Lacan formalizes this recurring moment, the endless repetition of this search, as the very structure of desire: $\$ \lozenge a$. This formula designates the incommensurability ($\lozenge$) of the barred (divided) subject ($\$$) to the object of its desire. Although in return for the loss of the object the subject is given a place in language, which seems to promise a fulfilment of desire, such fulfilment cannot be delivered, since the lost object resists final symbolization. Unconscious desire will therefore perpetually undermine the meanings imposed by language, subverting the symbolic and leading to endless figuration, a poetics of the unconscious.

Thus for Lacan the function of language is only seemingly communication: it has rather the function of trying to produce a social bond as a stable montage of symbolic and imaginary. But the symbolic order itself – apart from the illusory effects of consistency produced by the imaginary – is experienced as an alien force impinging from outside and it is for this reason that Lacan calls it 'the Other'. With the assumption of a name and place in the Other the divided subject comes into being as a relation between two signifiers: it exists for another subject only in a pre-existing social bond where all the possibilities of meaning have already been established. Yet the 'I' which speaks will always be governed by the discourse of the Other internalized in the unconscious, undermining the restricted possibility of meaning imposed by language. Where Freud sees this as coming about by means of the mechanisms of condensation and displacement, as he identified them first in dreams and the hysteric's discourse, Lacan translates these figures into the classical tropes of metaphor and metonymy. Metaphor, which is the substitution of one signifier for another, produces, as it pins together two signifying elements in unwonted juxtaposition, a superabundance of sense which can temporarily relieve the oppression of desire; metonymy is the movement from signifier to signifier in a pre-established world of sense, which, however, generates the continuing oppression of desire that cannot find representation itself except in the intervals between signifiers,[4] between the lines. The subject cannot be autonomous, for the figurality of language only provides provisional, ironic satisfaction; signification is only partial.

Yet the symbolic never stops inscribing itself, organizing every social relation and every discourse, in particular that of the sexual. For Lacan there is no sexual relation that can be inscribed in discourse. It is the traces of that non-inscription (as in Lear's 'The Owl and the Pussy-Cat') that we so eagerly pursue in discourse, filling the gap with our fantasies. An ideal sexual relation is impossible (in the unconscious the woman remains the mother, the woman who has everything – the libidinal pig of the poem), although it is necessarily pursued as that which promises the longed-for plenitude.

Freud works with the dualistic concept of a pleasure principle, where our acts are governed by the prospect of pleasure or unpleasure, and a reality principle, where through our encounter with the external world detours to and delays of satisfaction are enforced. Although there is an admission here that the two principles are interconnected, in that the central question of the modes of achieving satisfaction is implied in both, Freud's emphasis is on learning to distinguish the difference between the hallucinatory fulfilment of a wish and a reality-tested external world in which some measure of satisfaction is possible. The opposition of these two principles founders on the notion of pleasure as the satisfaction of a need and pleasure as grounded in fantasy. Because Freud made a final appeal to what he saw as the biological bedrock of the mind he was unable to find a link between satisfying needs and pursuing fantasies. His postulation of the death drive, Thanatos, as a principle of disintegration, on the one hand, and Eros, as a principle of integration, on the other, can be looked upon as an attempt to find a better foundation for his theory.

So what could be theoretically prior to these two principles? Out of what might they emerge? Instead of this dualism Lacan proposes a dialectic of need, demand and desire. The need is for nourishment (the realm of the real), demand is for the mother's absolute love (the imaginary), desire is for a fantasy, the mnemic traces of a lost object (the symbolic). In this new constellation the real of need is shown to be intersecting with the symbolic in an imaginary mode in order to achieve the detours of desire that Freud addressed. In allowing the real to produce effects upon both symbolic and imaginary, a dialectic between 'pleasure' and 'reality' can take place in discourse.

Discourse is the means by which human subjects forge new detours of desire. In his theory of the four discourses Lacan produces a series of formulaic models, discourse 'mathemes', whereby he analyses what happens when a subject speaks.[5] The four discourses are that of the Master, the University, the Hysteric, and the Analyst; between them they comprise all the possible unconscious relations that are brought into play at different moments in a so-called communication situation. They can be viewed as counter to Jakobson's model in that they demonstrate the impossibility and impotence of 'normal' communication. Instead of the structuralist emphasis on language as solely constituted by differences, what emerges is the uncanniness of discourse as that which, while aiming to forge and maintain a social bond, is continually undermined. Yet, paradoxically, according to Lacan, the discourses are nevertheless the only way in which a social bond can be maintained. Unlike Jakobson, Lacan does not take communication as the transmission of a stable message from one speaker to another, but starts out with the assumption that, as in the analytic situation, the relation of speaker to hearer is a relation of desire which is an *unconscious* structure determining both parties. All discourse is the 'discourse of the Other', by which Lacan means the order of language as a chain of signifiers which impinge from outside and produce the subject, not vice versa, the subject producing language, as in Jakobson's model. When Lacan later declares that 'the unconscious is the desire of the Other' he is precisely stressing that the unconscious is the result of speech that is addressed to the subject from elsewhere, from 'the other side', to use Alfred Kubin's coinage.

It is constitutive for every discourse that the subject appears only as represented by another signifier. To use a distinction developed by the linguist Émile Benveniste,[6] the grammatical term 'I', the subject of the enunciation (the unconscious), is not coterminous with 'me', the subject of the announced (the ego). What does this mean? Lacan's account of discourse shows that I am alienated in language, that when 'I' identify myself in discourse, this is always a partial identity – an identification – never a full one. I must make use of signifiers to be represented, to *be* at all, yet the signifier cannot represent my 'non-being', that for which I have no words. The subject of the announced, 'me', and the subject of the enunciation, 'I', are different positions for the speaking subject and it is split between them ($\$$). It is worth noting that the discourse formulas form a matrix in which the 'places' above and below the line are reduplicated in each discourse, but the 'terms' in those places rotate.

For Lacan there is no discourse without the following four terms: a field of unconscious knowledge which he calls S2; a master signifier, S1, which intervenes and sorts this field; the split subject, $\$$; and the *objet a*, an 'unspeakable' remainder, an excess produced by the discourse which Lacan calls '*plus-de-jouir*' and which can only be unsatisfactorily translated as 'surplus enjoyment'. That is to say, it is not an enjoyment that can be attained in the symbolic; it is 'unspeakable', beyond any possible satisfaction. Yet it is this remainder or excess which keeps the discourse going: if the discourse covered the real, there would be no movement.

Each of the four terms, knowledge (S2), the master signifier (S1), the split subject ($\$$), the object of desire (a), can occupy each of the discursive positions in turn and this is what distinguishes one discourse from another. Schematically, the places and terms are listed thus:

The positions		*The terms*	
agent	other	S1	the master signifier
truth	product	S2	knowledge
		$	the split subject
		a	object of desire

The place of the *agent* is that of the instance in whose name the discourse happens (on the left in the matrix), who speaks to *the other* (positioned to the right of the agent). Also part of the discourse is the effect produced by the agent's address to the other – the space of the *product* (below the bar). Whatever goes into this space is not a 'conscious' product that is deliberately aimed at by the agent of the discourse but rather the irreducible remainder of the discursive process that is structurally misrecognized by the agent. On the left below the bar is the *truth* of the subject, what the subject does not know it is saying. This truth, which is unconscious and actually determines the discourse, is never that which is transmitted to the other, and hence Lacan defines the relations between speaker and hearer, agent and other, above the bar, as 'impossible' communication. Since the address to the other is blocked, there is no channel for the desire that motivated it. There is a similar failure below the bar, for whatever the product of the discourse may be, it will always fail to match what is in the place of truth. This 'impotence' of the relation between product and truth induces the failure above the bar, of the agent's attempt to reach the other. It is the constant attempt to confront this double failure that constitutes the social bond, different in the case of each discourse.

The permutation of these terms among the four fixed positions produces the four discourses. Each of the discourses tends to turn into the other; all discourse turns through the system without anyone finally being the master of it, including the Master. That is to say, the terms are not fixed, as in Jakobson's model, but rotate, occupying variable positions. But even though one might not want to speak as Master, one cannot choose not to be heard as such, which is, above all, the problem of the analyst as 'subject-supposed-to-know'.

The discourse of the Master,

$$\frac{S1}{\$} \quad \frac{S2}{a}$$

which attempts to dominate the field of knowledge by imposing rigid canons of sense on the signifiers of the other, sifts out the object of desire as that which is excluded (under the bar). This is the prototype of the master/slave relation, where the signifier (S1) is in command, determining a certain kind of social bond. The master tries to appropriate the slave's knowledge in order to satisfy his desire. The master has rigidified the symbolic: S1 (in the place of the agent) legislates for a single meaning. But since the object of desire is excluded from the field of knowledge, the master's demand is impossible. The *objet a* stays under the bar, repressed. The surplus of meaning is kept inoperative in this discourse.

The modern variation of this discourse is the discourse of the University where impartial knowledge, universal reason, is in the place of the agent:

$$\frac{S2}{S1} \quad \frac{a}{\$}$$

This puts knowledge in the place of the master, masking the presence of the master as the truth of this discourse. Knowledge is idealized and objectified and taken as existing in its own right: the symbolic is taken to be in order as it is, as if all fact were neutral. The master signifier is now repressed, under the bar, concealed by the institutionalization of knowledge. Also addressed in this discourse is the object of science – the view from nowhere, the world completely objectified, stripped of its subjective meaning – becoming an object in which the subject does not recognize itself. The product of this discourse, misrecognized by the agent and excluded from the field of scientific knowledge, is the subject, now self-alienated as a direct consequence, a further result being that the object is denied its subjective significance.

So much for the discourses which maintain the structure of the always already-constituted social reality. What about the other two? Psychoanalysis as a technical praxis which specifically addresses the symptoms generated by the established order came into being through the discourse of the Hysteric:

$$\frac{\$}{a} \quad \frac{S1}{S2}$$

In the discourse of the Hysteric the position of the agent is occupied by the split subject, that is, subjective division is what is manifest and it is the subject thus divided against itself which addresses to the master signifier questions about the signifiers of identity offered to the subject by its culture. Lacan expresses this by the hysteric's question: 'Am I a man or a woman?' In the position of truth is *objet a*, the *plus-de-jouir*, the unassimilable object which is the cause of the subject's division. The product of this questioning of the master signifier by the divided subject is a knowledge of the discursive arrays of a given culture, the effect of which is evidenced by the hysterical symptom, but it is a knowledge which is powerless to intervene in them.

In the discourse of the Analyst,

$$\frac{a}{S2} \quad \frac{\$}{S1}$$

the position of truth is occupied by knowledge, but here it is specifically unconscious knowledge where the play of signifiers in the Other is not subject to the master signifier (this is the only discourse where S1 and S2 are separated, that is, the master signifier is no longer able to dominate knowledge). This is reflected in the free association of psychoanalysis which is not supposed to be determined by the conscious choice of the subject. It is this play of signifiers in S2 that determines the object of desire, *a*, which is in the position of the agent. In analysis the analyst seeks to adopt this position, continually evoking by means of his interventions the focus of this object as determined by unconscious knowledge, the configuration of S2. But the analyst does not hold the key to the subject's unconscious; his or her task is to get the analysand to recognize the relation between his or her symptoms and the knowledge they conceal. To achieve this, the analyst punctuates the analysand's discourse with monosyllables, interpretations and, in Lacanian analysis, deliberate cuts which mark the end of the session. As *objet a*, the analyst seeks to locate her/himself in the place of the analysand's desire. The discourse of the Analyst is the only one in which unconscious truth can function as knowledge. Truth is not some kind of mystical insight or permanent self-knowledge, but a narrative which pertains to the subject in all its particularity. This is the only discourse in which the *objet a* as a fragment of the real is in a place where it can effect the movement of signifiers, precipitating as product of the S1 a new master signifier of identification that is produced by the subject itself rather than imposed by the established order designated by the master. Truth will always be an enigma, since it is impossible to know everything consciously that is known unconsciously, and hence, according to Lacan, can only be 'half-said'. Nevertheless, this is the safeguard against the possibility of *jouissance* flooding over the boundaries of the symbolic, what Freud was afraid of when he wrote *Beyond the Pleasure Principle.*[7]

So how might this connect with a Lacanian view of the function of literature and the arts? As discussed above, Freud's psychoanalytic aesthetics offer images of consolation as a compromise between a wish and its renunciation. His focus is mainly on the author as the *agent provocateur* of this process. Lacan shifts the emphasis firmly onto the reader/spectator. Psychoanalysis cannot directly tell us about the unconscious signification of art and literature, but it might tell us why a given work produces an effect in the reader. In the discourse of the analyst, knowledge is in the place of the unconscious, no longer the property of the master, whether he or she be the analyst or the artist/writer: to speak of the unconscious as a discourse means not to locate it in a single agency. What is being mobilized in art and analysis is an unconscious which goes beyond the boundaries of the single subject. Thus the discourse of the analyst is also the discourse of art, for in both, the object *a* – that which designates the surplus beyond the symbolic – remains to be wrestled with as the cause of desire.

How, then, can art create pleasure for others? We know Freud's view: the aesthetic element overcomes resistance, preparing for access to the unconscious fantasy. What we might call, after Friedrich Nietzsche, the Apollonian function of the image can protect us from the Dionysian. But whereas Freud is concerned with the function of the image, Lacan dwells on the problem of the (lost) object. Lacan thus introduces a dimension of (real) lack into the aesthetic. The image serves as a screen for the object which the subject desires to look at. There is a difference between (conscious) seeing and (unconscious) looking. To see concerns the image which gives us pleasure: to look has a relation to the object which is lacking. This search produces anxiety instead of pleasure, because the real object is unrepresentable. It cannot be represented by an image, since it is what is lacking in the image. In his seminar 'Of the gaze as *objet petit a*', Lacan speaks of the dialectic between the eye and the gaze (the work's otherness regarding us). Art, he says, combines the lure of the gaze (the *trompe l'oeil*) and its power to tame (the *dompte-regard*).[8] It tames (rather than consoles, as in Freud) because it encourages 'renunciation', by making the spectator/reader simultaneously aware of desire and lack. It encourages sublimation rather than idealization because the ideal object, being unrepresentable, is shown not to be hidden but absent.

The veil of beauty, the lure, conceals the lacking object, and thus protects the one who looks. In Wordsworth's poem entitled 'Elegiac Stanzas'[9] the poet is aghast at the sight of George Beaumont's painting of the stormy sky over Peele Castle, which he remembers as an idyllic scene:

> So pure the sky, so quiet was the air!
> So like, so very like, was day to day!
> Whene'er I looked, thy Image still was there;
> It trembled, but it never passed away.

'In the fond illusion of [his] heart', this is the vision the poet would have painted, seeing in it 'the soul of truth' and a 'stedfast peace that might not be betrayed'. But the Apollonian vision has been succeeded by the Dionysian one of 'lightning, the fierce wind, and trampling waves'. As Immanuel Kant makes the sublime serve as a shield for terror,[10] so the poet allows the 'passionate Work' (which might be seen as the psychic work of poet/analyst and reader/analysand, as well as Beaumont's painting) to tame his totalizing grasp, renouncing the imaginary plenitude under the poetic, not-so-tame threat:

> And this huge Castle, standing here sublime,
> I love to see the look with which it braves,
> Cased in the unfeeling armour of old time,
> The lightning, the fierce wind, and trampling waves.

Pace Kant, the work of art betrays its own uncanniness. It provides a fantasy object, inciting the look, and lures us to search for what we cannot see in the 'real' painting outside the poem. It speaks of something beyond the visible, beyond pleasure, and beyond beauty.

> So once it would have been,– 'tis so no more;
> I have submitted to a new control:
> A power is gone, which nothing can restore;
> A deep distress hath humanized my Soul.

Wordsworth's 'Elegiac Stanzas' is a self-named poem about mourning and we know that it is also a mourning for the drowning of his brother John at sea. Nevertheless with this loss the poem also commemorates a more primal loss (a very Wordsworthian gesture), one in which even the most celebratory work of art and its reception participates, if we take a Freudo-Lacanian view of language.

The poet, dramatist, philosopher and historian Friedrich Schiller, confronting the idea of loss – for him the loss of an ideal past – distinguishes the poetry of the *naive* from that of the *sentimental* (in using these German terms he had in mind Goethe for the first and himself for the second). He thought thereby to make a philosophic contribution to genre in that he tried to separate what he saw as an unselfconscious,

unmediated relation to nature in which the real and the ideal
are, at least momentarily, at one (the *naive*), from a self-
conscious distanced one in which the poet is aware of his (symbolic) alienation (the *sentimental*). By Schiller's reckoning,
Wordsworth would have been a *sentimental* poet (the word in
German does not denote excessive indulgence in emotion, but
excessive reflectiveness), since he invariably writes in the past
tense, mourning what he no longer possesses. The sublime is a
way of transcending this dilemma, an attempt to bridge the
gap between the *naive* and the *sentimental*, which Schiller, the
Kantian, also undertakes. For the literary critic Harold Bloom,
on the other hand, the poetry of the sublime represents a manic
triumph over loss,[11] but nevertheless it is the 'strong poet'
that he admires: a strong poet is someone who is not afraid to
advance on his precursors, in Freud's case, by producing a
theory of the unconscious that steals a march on the poets'
own awareness of it.

The idealizing and superegoic elements of Wordsworth's
'Elegiac Stanzas' cannot obliterate the uncanny play of real,
imaginary and symbolic, respectively, the 'unfeeling armour
of old time', 'the gentlest of all gentle things' and 'the light
that never was'. This skirting round the lost object is reminiscent of Lacan's celebrated reading of Poe's 'The purloined letter',[12] whereby he turns a detective story into an allegory of
mourning. Likewise Lacan reads *Hamlet* as a play about the
inadequacy of mourning, as discussed in chapter 6, an allegory of blocked desire and of the act of mourning which finally unblocks it.

Putting together Freud and Lacan, the power of literature
and art might be seen to have a dual nature. For Freud, the
aesthetic factor resides in the capacity of the artist to transform his infantile material into something that by its complex
figuration offers a respite from privation and gives pleasure;
and it is obvious that Freud derives pleasure from the psychoanalysis of art and the artist, for all his honorific gestures
to the mysteries of both. For Lacan, art has more the function
of the analyst, its discourse offering itself as cause of desire
and raising an ethical dimension: the semblance of the (lost)
object, like the analyst's equivocal interpretation, provokes

and opposes the inertness of the fantasy, producing the un-canny effect. There is suffering because of the desire of the Other, which sets the limit to the subject's desire. There is an obligation to otherness, but also to not giving up one's desire. Discourse is the endless mediation whereby conflictual de-sires contest the boundaries between real and symbolic.

6

The indirections of desire: Hamlet

In his 'Desire and the interpretation of desire in *Hamlet*', Lacan uses *Hamlet* as an allegory both of blocked desire and of the act of mourning which unblocks it.[1] He sees Hamlet as the man who has 'lost the way of his desire' and who can thus represent the tragedy of human desire in general. The graphs of desire that Lacan appends in a footnote are formalizations of the founding of the unconscious and paradigmatically illustrate Hamlet's predicament in terms of the vicissitudes suffered by a subject upon its entry into language.[2] The graphs plot the way that the signifiers of language create the subject, who is dependent on the signifier for forging human relationships. Language cuts up the body, naming its different parts, reducing the body of *jouissance* to what the symbolic decrees. Although the subject may try to demand absolute satisfaction at the level of the (partial) drive, it will never achieve it. This dependence on the signifier prevents the subject from achieving total being; it has to pay for its entry by mortgaging 'that self-sacrifice, that pound of flesh'(p. 13).

In his readings of literary texts Lacan is interested in the same thing that interests him in the clinical encounter, namely, what it is that causes human beings to desire. If the short answer is language – which already establishes an analyst's credentials for taking a clinical look at the literary – then the long answer comes from each individual text, whether it be that of a living subject or a literary one. Lacan's answer to the question of Hamlet's desire is much longer than Freud's famous comments, though not as long as those of Ernest Jones, which run to a book.[3] Freud was interested in the whys and wherefores of Hamlet's vacillating desire and offered the outlines of a classic reading: 'Hamlet is able to do anything – except take vengeance on the man who did away with his father and took that father's place with his mother, the man who shows him the repressed wishes of his childhood realized'.[4] Jones, who took his cue from Freud, nevertheless significantly anticipated Lacan's account in pointing out the mother's contribution to the conflict, namely, 'her markedly sensual nature and her passionate fondness for her son'.[5]

Lacan's readings of literary texts are also clinical readings and therefore may not endear themselves to literary critics. Yet they are not clinical in the way that Freud undertook his readings of literary and artistic texts, believing that he was making manifest a latent meaning. Lacan's readings do not reconstruct a latent narrative from a manifest one and do not rush into taking the immediate familial constellations as determining the structure of the text. He asks questions which the Freudian reader had not thought of asking. This is equally true of his readings of other literary texts, such as of Poe's 'The purloined letter', Sophocles' *Antigone*, Plato's *Symposium* and the work of Joyce and the Marquis de Sade. Though these readings may not be literary in the commonly accepted sense, it can be argued that they concern themselves with the constitution of the subject in law and language, it being (poetic) language which founds the subject in the first place.

For Lacan, Hamlet's unarticulated question to his mother, 'What do you want?', is the subject's question to the Other about its desire. Prince Hamlet still sees himself as his mother's object rather than as her son, the future king: 'his fate is expressed in terms of a pure signifier, a level at which he is the reverse-side of a message that is not even his own' (p. 12): Hamlet's story is determined by a narrative, a signifying constellation that has been imposed upon him. The message that comes back to his question is truly enigmatic. Hamlet is caught in the desire of the mother, who conflates the symbolic phallus of kingship with the real phallus of Claudius, for the Queen wants both the power associated with the king as idealized object and the illicit enjoyment of a purely carnal relationship with Claudius, the adulterous brother. The Queen is in pursuit of her own loss, her own 'pound of flesh', and Hamlet, still in thrall to the (m)Other, wants to be it, her imaginary phallus.[6] Gertrude prevents Hamlet's appropriation of his symbolic position. As a result Hamlet cannot make the message his own; he is getting the wrong message from her, namely, that there is no need to be castrated, no need to make a sacrifice for entry into the symbolic.

Lacan's reading therefore differs sharply from Freud's since what is at stake is the mother's desire rather than Hamlet's. Hamlet is not just wrestling with desire *for* the (m)Other, but is endeavouring to find out the desire *of* the Other. In neurosis the Other is in command and leaves the subject out of step 'fast or slow, early or late' (p. 16), not knowing what desire to pursue or when to pursue it. Whatever Hamlet does, it is never at a time of his own choosing. Even when he sets up the Player Scene, Hamlet is unable to react to the King's demonstrable guilt. But when he is caught out in a sudden challenge to act, he does it precipitately, as in the killing of Polonius or the escape from the ship.

Because not all of the subject's being can go into language, a fantasy emerges as an imaginary filler. For Lacan, Ophelia is the key term in the play precisely because she is this fantasy. As Hamlet is the drama's principal subject, so Ophelia is its principal object because of the place she comes to occupy in Hamlet's desire, that of *objet a*, a fantasy of the phallus of which he feels deprived. The fantasy is 'ambiguous and para-doxical' because something is being *consciously* pursued, namely, a woman, Ophelia, who represents 'the end-term' of an *unconscious* desire, the phallus (p. 14). In pathological situations like that of Hamlet's, perverse desire breaks through at 'the level of the message', in symptomatic form, as Lacan will show in the incident where Hamlet, feigning madness, appears to Ophelia. In Hamlet's relation to her, Lacan discerns a shift from the structure of neurosis to a moment of perversion. Whereas in neurosis, as has been seen, the subject is dominated by its relation to time, in perversion the subject is out of time, fixated on whatever fetish it can find: 'the subject tries to get control of himself in the fantasy', searching there for what he has lost.

It is the revelation of the Queen's adultery and the undead King's injunction to kill the adulterer that make Ophelia null and void as a fantasy object for Hamlet. He is now doubly betrayed. He rejects Ophelia because he equates her with his mother: just as Gertrude has betrayed him with Claudius, so Ophelia has betrayed him to Polonius in acceding to her father's demand to stay away from her lover. For Lacan it is at this point that perversion takes over from neurosis, in which the fantasy, instead of being interlocked with the subject Hamlet, now appears as if estranged from him, 'tipped towards the object' (p. 22). This emerges in Ophelia's speech which describes how he stares, sighs and ruminates as if she were now dissociated from him, 'no longer a symbol signifying life' (p. 23). It is in these gestures, the 'message', that his perverse desire breaks through: thenceforth, and until her death, he treats her as a desecrated object, fit only for the brothel. He has lost the object that was the phallus for him: the fantasy has decomposed. Because Ophelia has moved across the boundary between inside and outside, subject and object, she has become uncanny for Hamlet.[7] Hamlet's own behaviour becomes uncanny as a result; his acts never seem to coincide with his desire. That an act should take place which will accord with the subject's desire is part of the illusion of the symbolic. In waiting for the symbolic's demand Hamlet behaves as if desire and act were seamlessly at one, as if the symbolic knew when anything should be done. But, as Lacan says, 'in the signifier there is nothing that guarantees the dimension of truth founded by the signifier' (p. 25). As is the general case, Hamlet's 'truth' escapes the signifier, because what he lacks is precisely the 'pound of flesh', the (symbolic) phallus.

Hamlet has chosen the path of self-destruction because he is not able to fulfil the Ghost's mandate in any other way. He is tempted into a fencing match with Laertes, a man of action who, unlike Hamlet, is prepared to revenge his father. Laertes represents the ideal ego, the mirror-image of the perfect other without lack: what Hamlet really wants is to overcome the

mirror rival (his 'foil', as the text makes clear). Although he
divines that the challenge is a trap of some kind, he ignores
the danger he suspects: 'he has entered into the game without, shall we say, his phallus' (p. 32). Laertes and Claudius
provide the instruments of death: thus, at the eleventh hour,
the Other has given him the weapon, when he has nothing
more to lose, when he is on the point of death, the final castration. At long last he is able to act on behalf of the symbolic,
identifying with the symbolic phallus instead of the imaginary one. There is here a poetics of the subject, unconsciously
realized: Hamlet has troped himself, placing himself in a position in which his proven capacity to act promptly can be put
to use; he is actively constituting himself as a subject by bringing his desire into the symbolic.

The first sign of an acceptance of symbolic castration occurs at the funeral of Ophelia. Here the rivalry with Laertes
shows itself for the first time, and, according to Lacan, is more
authentic than in the duel – since Hamlet initially fights with
a harmless weapon. But at Ophelia's funeral he leaps head-
long into the grave and struggles with Laertes over the body,
competing with him for the right and power to mourn. Because Ophelia is dead, he can assume his lack and speak with
symbolic power. The ostentation with which Laertes mourns
restores in Hamlet a sense of the worth of the rejected object,
now inaccessible and impossible. Lacan makes the clinical
observation that an impossible desire is what the obsessional
wants.

Thus *Hamlet* is not only a drama of blocked desire but also
of the mourning that is required to unblock it. In both mourning and melancholia, for Freud as for Lacan, there is a challenge to the subject's narcissistic investment in the lost object:
both states involve resistance to yielding up this investment
(see chapter 4 above). For Freud, the strategy for the melancholic was to 'incorporate' the lost object, to preserve its presence within as if it still existed: for Lacan, there is a reaction
to the gap or hole that appears in the real when the subject
loses its loved object. The subject's identification no longer
holds; the signifier on which the subject depended is no longer
available. The trauma of this loss forces a repetition of the

original entry into the symbolic, but the Other will not give an answer until the place is repurchased through a renewed acceptance of castration, the loss of the phallus (cf. Kristeva on forgiveness, pp. 49–50 above). Until then, as in psychosis, the subject will suffer an invasion of images, substitutes for the missing phallus. The phallus has to be mourned 'at the level of the *logos*' (p. 38), through an engagement with the symbolic, just as the dead have to be mourned through the social emphasis of ceremonial rites. As in tribal myth the disregard of formal ceremony brings the threat of ghosts and spectres, so too, failure to mourn the phallus, to accept castration, leaves both subject and the signifying system in disorder.

Lacan points out that *Hamlet* is marked throughout by its references to mourning, in particular, inadequate mourning. Mourning is a recurring theme in the play, yet the mourning itself is always insufficient. The formal rites have been curtailed or ignored: first, there is the murder of the King, who complains that he was denied the sacraments due to the dying; second, the 'o'erhasty marriage' of Gertrude and Claudius, which curtailed the mourning period; and third, the unceremonious burials of Polonius and Ophelia. In every case the rites are not enough, a repeated allegory of the failure to participate in a communal act that makes the subject's lack 'coincide with the greater *béance*, the point x , the symbolic lack' (p. 40). The focus of the play is thus the 'drama of desire' that takes place as a result of 'mourning and its demands' (p. 41). Lacan wants to relate the 'normal' pursuit of the lost object to its pathological pursuit in mourning, showing that a form of mourning is involved in every struggle with Oedipal desire. Not until mourning becomes adequate will the narcissistic investment that prevents Hamlet acting in his own time be surrendered. In Lacan's view, Freud's reading of *Hamlet* leaves out the necessary process of mourning. This entails the abandonment of imaginary plenitude in return for a place in the symbolic register, in which the subject's demand for love can once more begin to index itself. Since in *Hamlet* this is achieved only at the price of death, Lacan calls the play a 'tragedy of desire'.

In both *Oedipus Rex* and *Hamlet* the crime at the core of

the story intensifies the significance of mourning, for all subjects are guilty of Oedipal desire. In *Totem and Taboo* Freud
constructs a primal myth in order to explain how the law arose
from the endeavour to regulate this desire:[8] there was a murder by the sons of the primal father, who possessed all the
women, following which the guilt of the sons banded them
together under the taboo of incest. Lacan argues that in both
plays the tragic hero retraces the line from crime to law, but,
whereas in *Oedipus Rex* the crime is performed by a hero who
is 'completely innocent, unconscious and unaware' (p. 42), in
Hamlet the crimes committed by Claudius, those of regicide
and fratricide, are deliberate. The crime is against the King
and has the particular effect of denying him the opportunity
to pay the debt for his sins. Because of this impossibility he
reveals himself as the barred Other to Hamlet, as castrated
and yet unable to mourn. This is a negative poetic effect in
that the immortal centre of the symbolic, the dead king, is
missing and cannot be marked.

The guilt factor for Hamlet is thus intensified, unable as he
is to carry out the King's injunction. Lacan sees this predicament as a decadent form of the Oedipal situation, since there
is an unresolved unconscious conflict in the hero. Because of
the place that Claudius occupies in the Oedipal triad, Hamlet
is unable to mourn the loss of the phallus. For both Freud and
Lacan, the value of the phallus is tied up with the narcissism
of the subject, who, only when he finds himself under threat
of castration, will yield up a part of his being.

The tragedy of *Hamlet* revolves around the place and possession of the phallus. Lacan speaks of a 'phallophany' (a
showing of the phallus): the phallus momentarily shows itself from behind the 'veil' of language. Lacan describes the
accession to the symbolic as a journey of three stages: the
initial *castration* – the moment of vertigo produced by the
failure of the symbolic to provide a signifier for the real within
the subject (primal repression); the moment of *frustration* –
when the subject is in a state of imaginary complete submission to the symbolic law (the entry via the mirror stage); and
finally the moment of *privation* – in which the subject has 'to
situate himself in desire', that is, through mourning, to come

to a reorganization of his demand *vis-à-vis* his desire as symbolically defined.[9]

Lacan illustrates how this process is blocked in the play: Hamlet, in his relation to the phallus, is unable to proceed through these stages. There is an over-idealization of the father as the product of the stage of frustration. Whenever he speaks of him it is in extravagant terms ('Hyperion to a satyr') whereby he avoids actually saying anything about him. Claudius, on the other hand, he derides and insults, for Claudius is not only the shameless impostor occupying the throne, but possesses a real phallus that is enjoyed by Gertrude. What confounds Hamlet is that the phallus is 'out of place in terms of its position in the Oedipus complex' (p. 50), since the very place he wishes to fill is already illicitly occupied by Claudius. Hence the lawful and unlawful phallus are embodied in the one person. Hamlet cannot strike Claudius because he represents the completion that Hamlet wants to be for the mother: this completion must be there because this is where Gertrude finds it with Claudius. The (m)Other is showing no lack, and this is the essential cause of Hamlet's inability to act. He cannot conclude the Oedipal journey. No mourning is possible because there is apparently nothing to mourn. Lacan notes that Polonius is made into a proxy for what Hamlet cannot accomplish directly, namely, to strike at the phallus. Hamlet's remark 'I took thee for thy better', normally interpreted as 'I took thee for Claudius', can also signify 'I killed thee instead of thy better'. The killing of Polonius can thus be read as an act of unconscious intention, another of the ambiguous situations that allow Hamlet to act promptly; it is the very uncertainty about what is behind the arras, what is veiled, that allows him to act.

Finally, Lacan relates the phallus to two moments in the play. The first moment is Hamlet's remark about the corpse of Polonius, 'The body is with the king but the king is not with the body.' Replacing the word 'king' with the word 'phallus', Lacan now reads it as 'the body is with the phallus, but the phallus is not with the body' (p. 52), that is to say, the *jouissance* is vested in the body, but the body has been made to yield up its *jouissance* . The second moment is Hamlet's comment to

Guildenstern: 'The king is a thing . . . Of nothing'. The king, supposedly at the centre of the symbolic, does not have possession of the phallus, he has no-thing.

In this reading the literary and clinical have come together, fused through the poetics of the subject's mutations of identity, literary at the level of language, character and dramatic structure, and clinical in its analysis of the constitution of the subject in the dialectic of desire and drive.

7

Inscribing the body politic: Robert Coover's Spanking the Maid

Spanking the Maid [1] is a text that asks how the law can encompass the heterogeneity of the living body as law and body contend in an endless discourse. It is a story is about two characters, a master and a maid, caught in a repetitive cycle of law, transgression, guilt and punishment. Their interchange demonstrates graphically what happens when discourse is reduced to a deadlock by its purely imaginary dimension. The maid comes and goes daily, wearing her uniform, bringing her mop, brushes, bucket and broom – her 'paraphernalia', to speak with the text – preparing to install order in the master's bedroom and bathroom:

> She enters, deliberately, gravely, without affectation, circumspect in her motions (as she's been taught), not stamping too loud, nor dragging her legs after her, but advancing sedately, discreetly, glancing briefly at the empty rumpled bed, the cast-off night-clothes. She hesitates. No. Again. She enters. Deliberately and gravely, without affectation, not stamping too loud, nor dragging her legs after her, not marching as if leading a dance, not keeping time with her head and hands, not staring or turning her head either one way or the other ... As she's been taught. (p. 9)

Yet each day she comes to do her task, she somehow succeeds in creating disorder: she arrives late, or at the wrong moment, or without some essential, or something is slightly out of place ('he watches her place the pillows on the bed upside down', p. 37), or grossly out of place ('at the foot on the clear crisp sheets there is a little pile of wriggling worms, still coated with dirt from the garden,' p. 72). Each day the master wakes up from a troubling dream, rises reluctantly, struggles to assume his master-function at her entry, and staggers to the bathroom; each day, aided by a Victorian handbook and a pornography manual, he doles out instruction and chastisement.

But somehow the text and protagonists are at odds with each other: for although ostensibly and by their own account both master and maid are united in the task of attaining perfection, the maid-text's function is to bring desire and disorder into the master-text:

> 'What, what?' he yawns, and rolls over on his side, pulling the blanket over his head. She snatches it away . . . She stuffs her drawers hastily behind her apron bib, knocks over the mop bucket, smears the mirror, throws the fresh towels in the toilet, and jerks the blanket away again. 'I'm sorry, sir,' she insists, bending over and lifting her skirt. 'I'm sure I had them on when I came in . . .' (p. 97)

'To begin with, whose obsession is this?' one reviewer asks, answering that Coover 'gives us the voice of an imagined author, an author obsessed'.[2] But it would seem to be a voice which desires an equally obsessed reader, one who will get caught up in the perverse pleasure of the text. Indeed, this text could be taken as paradigmatic for one that requires a Barthesian erotics of reading, yielding unexpected pleasure, being, one might say, full of gaps, both formal, as lack and excess of plot, and thematic, as giving sometimes glimpses, sometimes expanses of the body.[3]

Who speaks, from what place, and to whom? What kind of discourse is going on here? Where to begin? One might try with Freud's essay 'A child is being beaten',[4] for instance, since the master and maid's relationship revolves around a beating fantasy. And indeed a variation of the fantasy turns up in the master's dreams, 'a teacher he once had who, when he whipped his students, called it his "civil service"' (p. 11), or was it 'sibyl service' (p. 32), or maybe 'civil severity' (p. 56). According to Freud, this kind of ('civil-service') fantasy in its various trans-formations is a fundamental fantasy, transindividually inscribed in the unconscious – a legacy of the child's Oedipal journey. The fantasy has three phases with three subject-positions that vary according to where the child subjectively places itself in the beating scenario. The three subject-positions are aggres-sor, victim and observer: (1) 'My father is beating the child whom I hate'; (2) 'I am being beaten by my father'; and (3) 'A child is being beaten'.[5] In the second phase – deeply repressed and hence a reconstruction in analysis – the child feels 'a con-vergence of the sense of guilt and sexual love' towards the father, which '*is not only the punishment for the forbidden geni-tal relation, but also the regressive substitute for that relation,* and from this latter source it derives the libidinal excitation which is from this time forward attached to it'.[6] In the master and maid's 'civil-service' fantasy these positions are inter-changeable, and hence the reader can insert herself in the fan-tasy wherever she likes, with her position disconcertingly unstable within the various scenarios.

The master's and maid's libidinous pleasure also includes her daily attention to his bodily needs as she follows his moist trail from bedroom to bathroom and back. Indeed, the damp-sheets-and-towels theme runs right through the text:

> But on that road, on the floor of the bathroom, she finds a damp towel and some pyjama bottoms, all puddled together, like a cast-off mop-head. (p. 13)

> What she really wants is to get him out of the sheets he's wrapped in, turn him over (he seems to have imbibed an un-healthy kind of dampness). (p. 100)

Moreover, this process of infantilization, this narcissistic in-vestment of certain bodily parts, applies as much to her as to him:

> she can never remember (for all the times he has explained it to her) why it is that Mother Nature has chosen that particu-

lar part of her for such solemnities. [. . .] Well, certainly it has always been neat and clean as he's taught her, that's the only thing she's never got wrong, always washing it well every day in three hot lathers, letting the last lather be made thin of the soap, then not rinsing it all or towelling it, but drying it over brimstone. (pp. 67–8, p. 69)

The positions of master and maid cross over: the polymorphous perverse plays itself out in both as they veer between anal and phallic, constantly staging and restaging a confusion of pleasure and guilt:

she advances, sedately and discreetly across the gleaming tiles to the bed, and tucking her dress and apron, pulling down her flannelette drawers, bends over the foot of it, exposing her soul's ingress to the sweet breath of morning. (p. 39)

'O! I beg your pardon, sir!' 'A dream,' he explains huskily, as his erection withdraws into his pyjamas like a worm caught in the sun, burrowing for shade. (p. 56)

So what kind of discourse is going on here? 'Maybe it's some kind of failure of communication', says Coover, 'a mutual failure. Is that possible? A loss of syntax between stroke and weal? No, no, even if possible, it is unthinkable' (p. 65). Not at all, says Lacan, 'it is speech functioning to the full, for it includes the discourse of the other in the secret of its cipher'.[7] The other turns out to be the big Other, law and desire as inscribed in language. The master is not a master after all. He may think that by modelling himself on the manuals he is serving some higher end:

All life is a service, he knows that. To live in the full sense of the word is not to exist or subsist merely, but to make oneself over, to *give* oneself: to some high purpose, to others, to some social end, to life beyond the shell of the ego. (pp. 24–5)

But in the Other scene, that of his nightly dreams, the letters which prescribe the higher end turn out to be interchangeable. The conscious and unconscious levels of language coincide with the split function of the master as he lives out his subjectivity

throughout day and night. In the night the poetics of the unconscious play havoc, turning 'utility' into 'futility' (p. 11), 'order' into 'odor' (p. 39), 'puzzle' into 'pizzle' (p. 95), 'hard part'
into 'heart part' (p. 66), 'morning' into 'mourning' (p. 85), 'hymnody' into 'humidity' (p. 56), 'higher ends' into 'hired ends' (p.
101). In the day the master cites from his Puritan-style manuals and lectures on 'those two fairies, confusion and disorder.
Method and habit, rather . . .' (pp. 87–8). The subject receives
its own message back, one part of the subject sending it to another. Humidity, damp sheets, sperm, are at odds with hymnody, the supposed perfect harmony of the social system, the
religious society, the art of hymn-making. Hymnody has humidity in it when it should be all the book spells out. The subject confronts its message from the Other: while consciousness
is trying to establish a world of order, the unconscious is dis-
rupting that order by what will not fit into it.

As the maid sets about her morning's duties, she models
herself on John Keble's poem 'Morning' (1827), 'the trivial
round, the common task . . . will furnish all she needs to ask'
(p. 13), and on George Herbert's 'The Elixir':

> '*Oh, teach me, my God and King, in all things thee to see, and what
> I do in any thing, to do it as for thee!*' she sings out to the garden
> and the room, feeling her heart lift like a sponge in a bucket. '*A
> servant with this clause makes drudgerie divine: who sweeps a room
> as for thy laws, makes that and the action fine.*' (p. 14)

For his part the master models his conduct on Victorian hand-
books and on the 'manuals' (p. 61) as variously represented in
the pornographic writings of the time:

> The proper stretching of a bull's pizzle, for example, this can
> occupy him for hours. . . . Or the fabrication of whipping chairs,
> the index of duties and offences, the synonymy associated with
> corporal discipline and with that broad part destined by Mother
> Nature for such services. (pp. 78–9)

> 'If domestic service is to be tolerable, there must be an atti-
> tude of habitual deference on the one side and of sympathetic
> protection on the other.' (p. 33)

For the master and maid these two complementary Puritan discourses unite to become a fantasized place of knowledge and truth, a would-be symbolic order of language and law, giving the two subjects the illusion of being in control of the very world which has enslaved them. Maid and master assume the words of the Other as if they were their own, 'as though once and for all', as the text says with each of the maid's abortive entrances. To the extent that they hold this illusion of being in control of the very system that placed them, they are in the imaginary, the mirror-world of the ego and its identifications. To inhabit the symbolic, to accede to language as the discourse of the Other, is to accept that language speaks of the loss that lies behind the earliest moments of symbolization, and that language, far from making good this loss, is no more than the site where desire can circulate. The symbolic covers over the inevitability of lack through the continual shifting of the signifier. The arbitrariness of the linguistic sign, apparently meaning what it says, ensures that neither maid nor master can speak of what they want except by means of parapraxes and punned images. They are already constituted by an order which goes beyond their imaginary interaction, even though they think it is still outside and has yet to 'get in': sometimes, when 'she presents to him that broad part preferred by him and Mother Nature for the invention of souls', for 'his disciplinary interventions', 'she hopes more has got in than is leaking out' (pp. 96, 25, 90).

However, the imaginary-cum-symbolic relation between master and maid is not immune to real effects – traumatic returns of the repressed – which the two recognize and interpret according to the manuals, where they find the appropriate punishment. These effects are the consequence of their doomed quest for consistency and perfection – 'perhaps today then . . . at last!' (p. 102). Since the maid is always aided by the various resistances coming from the real, she does not need to employ too many strategies to undermine this 'higher end':

> It never ends. Making the bed, she scatters dust and feathers afresh or tips over the mop bucket. Cleaning up the floor, she

> somehow disturbs the bed. Or something does. It's almost as if it were alive. Blankets wrinkle, sheets peek perversely out from under the spread, pillows seem to sag and puff all by themselves if she turns her back, and if she doesn't, then flyspecks break out on the mirror behind her like pimples, towels start to drop, stains appear on her apron. 'If she hasn't forgotten it!' She sighs, turns once more on the perfidious bed. (p. 82)

> She finds herself wishing she could make the bed once and for all: glue down the sheets, sew on the pillows, stiffen the blankets as hard as boards and nail them into place. (p. 83)

But the 'manual' furnishes no account of the origins of these effects caused by the real breaking through the gaps in the symbolic, by brute existence making its presence felt. The real is what 'leaks out' or drops off, beginning with a subject's earliest encounter, the separation from the mother's body: the real appears as the subject is thrown into life, and henceforth acts as an obstacle to the pleasure principle, a remainder and reminder of past and future fragmentation. These remainders, the 'abjects', to use Julia Kristeva's term, are elements of drive that have escaped repression and which preserve in the body what was there before the initial separation:

> Abjection preserves what existed in the archaism of pre-objectal relationship, in the immemorial violence with which a body becomes separated from another body in order to be – maintaining that night in which the outline of the signified thing vanishes and where only the imponderable affect is carried out. To be sure, if I am affected by what does not yet appear to me as a thing, it is because laws, connections, and even structures of meaning govern and condition me. That order, that glance, that voice, that gesture, which enact the law for my frightened body, constitute and bring about an effect and not yet a sign.[8]

Although these archaic moments have never been symbolized, they continue retroactively to produce traumatic effects, resulting in compulsive repetition. Whenever human beings take the symbolic too explicitly, expecting a precise fit between knowledge and being, the failure of the symbolic produces an answer from the real. The more exaggerated the law, the wilder the drive, and the bigger the gaps in which the real can make itself felt. The maid's 'abjection' is a return to those moments when the symbolic is hard to apply, when there is ambiguity, disorder, terror of disintegration. The master in the text meets these moments with the perennial shout of '"What? WHAT – ?"'

The 'pseudo-objects'[9] which the master and maid find and expect to find in the master's bed may be seen as figurations of the abject – insistent unconscious contents which return and force the subject to repeat its failed encounter with the real: 'no matter how much sunlight and fresh air she lets in, there's always this little dark pocket of lingering night which she has to uncover' (p. 28). Yet the bed is also the site where the subject expects to enjoy its fantasies and avoid the real: 'the spread is askew once again like a gift coming unwrapped' (p. 58). The bed is the text's most ambiguous object:

> She turns with a glad heart to her favourite task of all: the making of the bed. Indeed all the rest of her work is embraced by it, for the opening and airing of the bed is the first of her tasks, the making of it her last. Today, however, when she tosses the covers back she finds, coiled like a dark snake near the foot, a bloodstained leather belt. She starts back. The sheets, too, are flecked with blood. Shadows seem to creep across the room and the birds fall silent. Perhaps, she thinks, her heart sinking, I'd better go out and come in again . . . (p. 19)

> The other part is what she keeps finding in the bed. Things that oughtn't to be there, like old razor blades, broken bottles, banana skins, bloody pessaries, crumbs and ants, leather thongs, mirrors, empty books, old toys, dark stains. Once, even, a frog jumped out at her. (p. 28)

In their tussle with law and order, the master and maid each display the lurid symptoms of their trapped desire. The master's – 'stout engine of duty [. . .] a whip, a cane, a cat-o'-nine-tails, a bull's pizzle, a hickory switch, a martinet, ruler, slipper, a leather strap, a hair-brush' (p. 45), and that perennially wilt-ing erection which 'dips back into his pyjamas like a frog diving for cover – indeed it has a greenish cast to it in the half-light' (pp. 93–4). The maid's – her straying flannel drawers, 'at least she's remembered her drawers today: she's wearing them round her ankles. He sighs as she shuffles out' (p. 65), and her seductively twitching flesh: 'the two raised hemispheres upon which the blows from the birch rod have fallen begin (predictably) to make involuntary motions both vertically and horizontally [. . .] The weals criss-cross each other on her enflamed posteriors like branches against the pink clouds of dawn' (pp. 42–3).

It seems as if there is a perfect match between the master as punishing authority and the maid as guilty victim. However, the master's regular grumble, '"I wonder if you can appreciate . . . how difficult this is for me"' (p. 39), although ludicrous at the level of the story, is perhaps not so ludicrous at the level of the (psychoanalytic) plot, for, although to all intents and purposes the 'discourse of the Master' appears to prevail (see chapter 5 above), in that, as the reader of the manuals, he is in the supposed place of knowledge, he avows that he gets no pleasure from his mastery, and this the text intermittently confirms:

> Not that he enjoys all this punishment, any more (he assumes, but it doesn't matter) than she does. No, he would rather do just about anything else – crawl back into bed, read his manuals, even take a stroll in the garden. (p. 49)

Even though it is the maid who is in the submissive position, it is the master seemingly who has to produce the knowledge and labour for their perverse pleasure. But is it only the discourse of the Master that we hear? In Lacan's concept of discourse what is at stake is the unconscious structure of the relations which constitute the social bond and make speech possible: discourse assigns the subject a place from which it is in a position to speak to another subject (see chapter 5). Ostensibly, the master speaks to the servant within a Puritan order ('the duty of a servant is to be obedient, diligent, sober, just, honest, frugal, orderly in behaviour, submissive and respectful towards her master', p. 34), and the maid-servant is reduced to the mode of the master's knowledge. But what

actually dominates is the hysterical discourse of the maid, using the term 'hysterical' in Lacan's sense of the discourse of
the Hysteric, as paradigmatic for any subject posing the question of its subjectivity and demanding that the Other produce
the necessary knowledge for her or his pleasure. It is plain
that in the text the maid is refused the right to speak:

'What? *What?!* Answering back to a reproof – ?' (p. 52)

'You may speak when spoken to . . . unless it be to deliver a
message or ask a necessary question.' (pp. 35–6)

Here it would seem as if the maid is spoken by the master. Yet
she is far from being reduced to the knowledge of the master,
for, as the text amply shows, it is her behind which provides
the site of knowledge, it is her 'blank ledger' (p. 54) on which
the repressed desire is being constantly written and which
furnishes the symptoms so extravagantly figured by a text
which constantly preoccupies the master:

Sometimes, especially late in the day like this, watching the
weals emerge from the blank page of her soul's ingress like
secret writing, he finds himself searching it for something, he
doesn't know what exactly, a message of sorts, the revelation
of a mystery in the spreading flush . . . in the dew-bejewelled
hieroglyphs of cross-hatched stripes. (pp. 86–7)

In their commingled master/hysteric discourse there is an exaggerated upholding of the law and an exaggerated stimulation of desire. Their wilful game takes the form of an attempt
to match desire to the law, and events reveal that the law of
the manuals is complicit with perverse desire. Their rigid commitment to the law (both the manuals, and the Bible as medi-
ated by the poets in the text), represents the fear that desire
might not be underwritten by the law, that 'true service' might
not be 'perfect freedom', as 'he has taught her' (p. 47).

Their game is characterized by the inscribing of the law
upon the body, an incessant inscription perpetrated upon 'that
broad part destined by Mother Nature for such solemnities'
(p. 54). One of the most cherished philosophical ideas of lib-

eral humanism has been the hope of inscribing culture into nature on a higher level of consciousness, a 'second nature', according to Schiller, grounded in the belief that a higher order is already there in nature as a latent text . Nature includes within it a second nature, a higher synthesis of desire and law, accessible to the individual if only he will yield himself up to this 'higher end' (this categorical imperative). Wordsworth can be co-opted here and indeed might have served as yet another manual for master and maid:

> Praise to the end!
> Thanks to the means which Nature deigned to employ;
> Whether her fearless visitings, or those
> That came with soft alarm, like hurtless light
> Opening the peaceful clouds; or she may use
> Severer interventions, ministry
> More palpable, as best might suit her aim.[10]

The 'blank page' upon which the master performs his 'interventions' is certainly palpable. He is chastising her in the place where the soul is initially lodged, where sexual reproduction takes place. One of the text's continual jokes is the many references to birds and bees, traditionally made to figure sexual knowledge:

> Bees are humming in the garden and there's a crackly pulsing of insects, but the birds have fallen silent. (p. 35)

> Such a silence all about [. . .] it is not so inspiring as the song of the birds and even the bees seem to have ceased their humming. (p. 55)

> She strips the sheets and blankets off, shaking the dead bees into the garden. (p. 95)

But a knowledge of the reproductive processes of birds and bees will not reveal 'where babies come from', will not inscribe the knowledge that bodily parts, bodies are where souls begin. The images of the bottom make plain that the body, maliciously, this lower part of the body, becomes the 'higher end', the 'soul's ingress', the place where the soul begins: the bottom stands metonymically for the body, although it be its lowest, most ludicrous, most denigrated part. The image of writing becomes startlingly attached to it as the master is 'staring gloomily at her soul's ingress which confronts him like blank paper [. . .] a perversely empty ledger' (p. 81).

Spanking the Maid is a text about reading and writing, about wrestling with desire and drive. On every page there is a gap between word and deed (what the manuals and the Bible specify and what the two figures do), between labour and nature (the effort to restore order against the resistance of the real), between knowledge and being (the agreements of language against the actualities that disturb those agreements), between culture and nature (the specification of how the soul is to be invented against the involuntary spasms of the body and its attempt to 'come' into carnal knowledge). The conflicting effects these contradictions provoke are luridly inscribed in the text: 'her striped buttocks tremble and dance spontaneously [. . .] the whip sings a final time [. . .] and little drops of blood appear like punctuation, gratitude, morning dew' (pp. 61–2). 'Punctuation' is the inscribing from the manuals onto the body, 'the divine government of pain' (p. 89) producing what it must in order to make the body submit to what is marked out by the law. Hence, what produces the punctuation – the full stops, commas and dashes – is, inevitably, blood, suffering, repression, castration. But since images of dew and gratitude are also present as part of the text's wilful ambiguities, the positive aspects of an acceptance of law come into play. The drops of blood can turn into a sacrifice that could be made willingly, an 'amicable violence' (pp. 16 and 92) – a repeated oxymoron in the text – a kind of Brechtian consenting, perhaps easier if the society were different, if the laws were not tyrannical and oppressive.

And indeed the characters do experience moments of doubt about their 'divine government of pain' more ponderous, more general than the ones already cited:

> He wonders about his calling, how it came to be his, and when it all began: on his coming here? on *her* coming here? before that, in some ancient time beyond recall? And has he chosen

it? or has he, like that woman in his dream, showing him something that for some reason enraged him, been 'born with it, sir,
for your very utility'? (p. 30)

She wonders about the manuals, his service to them and hers
to him, or to that beyond him which he has not quite named.
Whence such an appetite? she shudders, groans, chewing helplessly on the pyjamas – so little relief? (pp. 98–9)

These meta-textual queries about the origins of desire and of
political and moral authority return repeatedly in the text.
They work as a frame for the continual tropings, the incessant
repetitions in many forms of the various themes. At the beginning of the story the images are at their most distinct, but
by the end everything runs together. As the text progresses,
because the repetitions have been so close and so incessant,
with the increasingly familiar words shifting their associative
links in every episode, the troping becomes more extravagant,
more carnivalesque. Every word that has been contiguous with
another can become its metonym; every word can evoke likeness in another and become a metaphor for it, however remote from it that likeness may be. This cumulative troping,
which moves to a climax in the last episode, itself performs
the text's critique of perverse law (as words shift their constraints), and of perverse desire (as meanings become dizzily
eccentric). But there is more than verbal play at stake, for this
is the explosion the text has intermittently prefigured, the
breakthrough of the fantasy that the text has been waiting
for:

The garden groans, quivers, starts, its groves radiant and throb-
bing. His teacher, no longer threatening, has withdrawn discreetly to a far corner with diagonal creases, where he is turning
what lilies remain into roses with his rumpled bull's pizzle: it's
almost an act of magic! Still his arm rises and falls, rises and
falls, that broad part of Mother Nature destined for such interventions dancing and bobbing soft and easy under the indul-
gent sun: "It's a beautiful day!" "What? *What?!* An answering
back to a reproof?" he enquires gratefully, taunting her with
that civility and kindness to an inferior, as – hiss – *Whap!* –
flicking lint off one shoulder and smoothing the ends of his

moustache with involuntary vertical and horizontal motions, he floats helplessly backwards ("Thank you, sir!"), twitching amicably yet authoritatively like a damp towel, down a bottomless hole, relieving himself noisily: *"perhaps today then . . . at last!"* (pp. 101–2)

Here is the other side of abjection, 'the moment when revelation bursts forth', *jouissance* (bliss) as Barthes has presented it:[11] the breakdown of the subject-object positions, the free play of the drive round the symbolic, the bliss of the text, the mingling of subject-positions, including that of author and reader. Everything becomes kaleidoscopic: instead of a repetitive structure there are psychotic shifts, instead of fantasy coming in its familiar inertness it comes with a shattering force that fragments the strict repetition. This, the end of the book, is a parody of closure, a mock epiphany, a refusal of the text to abandon its drive in the face of desire: 'his teacher, no longer threatening, has withdrawn discreetly', joining in the game of 'turning what lilies remain to roses' (p. 101). But is this all there is to it, the freeing of an anti-language within the old bourgeois ideology, a rejoicing in unbounded freedom?

In his book *The Political Unconscious* [12] Fredric Jameson argues that within the fragmented and alienated condition of society there is a collective impulse towards some kind of social bond. Since it is the function of ideologies to suppress the contradictions of history in order to reconcile the conflicting interests of oppressor and oppressed, a revolutionary criticism is required to reveal another kind of narrative in the text, the Utopian vision of the 'political unconscious'. In his deconstructive account of the work of Wyndham Lewis, Jameson operates with Gilles Deleuze's and Félix Guattari's concept of a discontinuous 'schizophrenic' text which invites the critic to recover a fragmented 'molecular' plot within an ordered 'molar' narrative.[13] According to Jameson, such a revolutionary criticism will reveal these contradictions and show to what extent the literary engages with the historical. Such a criticism will open up a 'realm of "originary" or creative language over against the daily practice of a degraded practical speech, the space of the sexual and archaic over against the reality-

and performance-principles of "*le sérieux*" and of adult life'.
Yet, Jameson continues,

> modernism not only reflects and reinforces such fragmenta-
> tion and commodification of the psyche as its basic precondi-
> tion, but . . . the various modernisms all seek to overcome that
> reification as well, by the exploration of a new Utopian and
> libidinal experience of the various sealed realms of psychic
> compartments to which they are condemned, but which they
> also reinvent.[14]

Here, then, is a direction for the text to be explored beyond
its binary opposition of a rigid symbolic against an anarchic
desire. Is there perhaps the possibility of reinscribing another
kind of order? If we read *Spanking the Maid* according to
Deleuze and Guattari we might find a 'molecular' plot between the anarchic play with language and beyond the para-
noiac narrative of relentless repetition. Can something be
glimpsed which breaks up the sterile circle of repetition (' "it's,
well, it's too repetitive",' says the maid, p. 28), something of a
social production of desire?

Coover's parodic text can be read as doing more than setting up ideological representations, more than, for example,
revealing how pornography battens upon bourgeois ideology.
It is not merely a latter-day attack on Puritanism, a gloomy
indictment of an aristocratic abuse of power; nor is it just taking an anarchic delight in the heterogeneous, the carnivalesque.
Even Deleuze and Guattari, while opting for a schizoanalytic
reading, tend to posit a negative hope, a belief in escape, a way
out of the system.

Although the parody clearly aims at the oppressiveness of
the system, particularly in its hold upon the consciousness of
master and maid caught up as they are in their unconscious
perverse complicities, there is also the maid's irrepressible hope.
This manifests itself, not only thematically, as a 'profound appetite for hope never quite stifled by even the harshest pun-
ishments' (p. 21), but also by the manner in which she invests
the scene with the joys and disappointments of her prospec-
tive labour. In each scene she initially endows the sensuous
world with the eagerness of her participations:

Ah! the morning sunlight comes flooding in over the gleaming tiles as though (she thinks) flung from a bucket. She opens wide the glass doors behind the curtains (there is such a song of birds all about!) and gazes into the garden, quite prepared to let the sweet breath of morning blow in and excite her to the most generous and efficient accomplishments, but her mind is still locked on the image, at first pleasing, now troubling, of the light as it spilled into the room: as from a bucket. . . . She sighs. She enters. With a bucket. (pp. 9–10)

As she remembers her constraints, momentarily forgotten in the pleasure of her sensuous experience, the bucket ceases to be the container for her joy; the 'defamiliarization' of the image, to speak with the Russian Formalists, is no longer operative, for as soon as she has once more to enter the room according to prescription, the text says 'buckets of light come flooding in (she is not thinking about this now)' (p. 10). The live image has virtually turned into a dead metaphor, lost its transparency, become opaque. Other images, invested with disappointment in her failures, momentarily retain their gloss, likewise showing themselves to be the result of a material production:

Running the maxims over in her head, she checks off her rags and brushes, her polishes, cleaning powders, razor blades, toilet paper, dustpans – oh no . . .! Her heart sinks like soap in a bucket. The soap she has forgotten to bring. (p. 38)

'Oh, teach me, my God and King, in all things thee to see, and what I do in any thing, to do it as for thee!' she sings out to the garden and the room, feeling her heart lift like a sponge in a bucket. (p. 14)

Thus, in the margins of the text one might perceive a hope for pleasure in labour, coupled with joy in nature, linked to images of work, rather than to ideological images of nature as 'sweet breath of morning' (pp. 14 and 39), which the text produces in such abundance. The maid works 'as though lifted by the tasks before her'; she is heard 'walking quickly back and forth, flinging open the curtains and garden doors, singing to herself' (p. 33). The rhythms of the text go along with her service, suggesting that under more favourable circumstances tasks *could* be something that the body might do singing. In this sense the text sustains a Herbertian view, its formal rhythms bespeaking a pleasure in order within a more successful society, one where the ideal in George Herbert's poem is not that of an outdated Puritan to be mocked at for equating God's service with freedom, but that of someone who might provide a way for translating the idea of God into social hope. The text might be seen as asking 'What is worthy in repression (in "amicable violence")?' According to D. H. Lawrence, nothing at all. He scoffed at the antics of a society which allowed the gorgeous Hester Prynne to parade the embroidered letter of her sin for all to see, calling it a triumph of the sensual over the spiritual, dubbing Hawthorne as one of the creators of false myths, one who 'knew disagreeable things in his inner soul' and was 'careful to send them out in disguise'.[15] The postmodern writer plays out social and political repression without any need to send disagreeable things out in disguise; according to Foucault, pleasure returns in any case as the triumphant return of the repressed at the periphery of power, thus counteracting oppression at multiple points of resistance.[16] For Jean-Jacques Rousseau, on the other hand, if the law is not upheld and renewed, the body politic, like the human body, begins to die from its birth, bearing in itself the causes of its destruction.[17] In *The Social Contract* he expressed the hope that the subject will accede to all laws, even those against its own inclination, but, if not, punishment would be needed to sustain repression, the subject 'forced to conform to wills that are not his own'.[18] Repression, then, is the inevitable price of being social: the body politic must be inscribed. But need the inscribing be so drastic? One might say that to be politic is also to be tactful, prudent, judicious about how bodies fit into societies, that society might accept tactful, that is ambiguous, fictitious, imaginative and mythic adjustments, such as Robert Coover's text suggests in the margins.

Spanking the Maid is a seductive and 'knowing' text. Through its figures, its chronic and playful slips, its rhythms, and the constant struggle of its characters with words, it performs and enacts the illusory literalness of language. As the hysteric's discourse, in which both master and maid are implicated, the text raises over and over again explicitly and implicitly the question of subjectivity. As the master's discourse, in which both characters are also implicated, the text represses knowledge and drives knowledge into self-reference; endless rumination about being serves only to obliterate being. As the analyst's discourse the text poses enigmas and bears on the reader as analysand: it challenges her or him to choose her or his subject-position and raises the problem of whose fantasy, the author's or the reader's, the text so insistently provokes. The reader is called upon repeatedly to enter the text – just as the maid enters the room each day – and take part in the struggle between knowledge and being, the knowledge that 'the cure' lies in working through the fantasy, on the one hand, acknowledging the interdictions of language and, on the other, allowing what is left out to circulate in discourse. In raising the question of subjectivity the text also participates in clinical analytic discourse and opens up the question of who speaks, from what place and to whom, posed by the literary and psychoanalytic discourses alike, neither of which can ever answer unequivocally.

8

What does Woman want?: The Double Life of Véronique

In Krzysztof Kieslowski's film[1] the question of subjectivity comes up again most forcefully in an exploration of the lives of two women. The film concerns significant differences in the experiences of these women, born at the same moment, one in Poland, one in France. They are identical in appearance, have the same musical talent, suffer from the same heart disease, have lost the mother at an early age and are brought up by a tender, caring father. The differences manifest themselves in their relation to their beautiful singing voice, their lovers and their familial figures.

One of the problems of deciphering *The Double Life of Véronique* is to decide what elements belong to an inventive fantasy tale with a mixture of traditional and modern Gothic features – the double or *Doppelgänger*, telepathic communion, the death of a beautiful singing woman (stories by E. T. A. Hoffmann and Thomas Mann come to mind),[2] the role of puppets (Hoffmann again, and perhaps Heinrich von Kleist)[3] – and what elements belong to an unconscious search by a (male) director for what Woman wants. The film taps into the Romantic tradition, making a puzzling return to the nineteenth-century topos of the double, raising the question of whether there might be a reading of this phenomenon not so historically bound.

The film is in two parts, taking place in Poland and France respectively, dealing with the life of each woman in turn: it presents a model of the self not quite settled in one place, one time and one identity. At moments each woman divines the existence of her twin. The doubles syndrome is here startlingly presented in two modes. First, as a sign of a question about the being of each woman: 'I feel that I am not alone', says the Polish Veronika, for here the double is experienced as a psychic shadow, covering the loss of something enigmatic. Second, for the French Véronique, the doubling is experienced as a psychic division, a split: 'All my life I was in two places at once', she says.

At a first approach, what binds the two parts together, then, are these parallel structures, to which more random features may be added. Like other films loosely related to this genre (*Death in Venice*, *Don't Look Now*), omens of impending doom manifest themselves in a semi-surreal mode in each part of the film. In Part 1, a larger-than-life statue of Lenin (the great father-figure) is being transported in a lorry and looms into view like some uninvited stone guest, momentarily blocking the path of the first Véronique; later, a sudden collision with someone fleeing from a riot, violently knocks her bundle of music sheets to the ground, scattering them about. In Part 2, the bleached white metal husk of a car, damaged and dented by a terrorist attack, is lifted away by a crane, observed by the second Véronique and her lover-to-be. Also in each part of the film an old woman crosses a road, bent over a stick, walking very slowly: the first Véronique wants to help her, while the second gives only a passing glance, a difference in their response that gathers enigmatic retrospective meaning.

What, then, might be the significant differences in the being of the two women, already indicated above? Why the 'double life'? Any attempt to answer the 'why' question will have to take account of the remarkable presentation of two different types of woman, achieved through distinguished acting (by one actress in the double role) and imaginative direction. As the first Véronique, living in Poland, Irene Jacob presents the image of a woman moving back and forth from serene confidence to ecstatic fervency. She lives with her father, who fulfils a maternal function, instead of introducing his daughter to the field of desire. This Véronique exists only in the moment, rejoicing in the fall of rain and other sensuous phenomena of the here and now. In the first shot following the titles we see her singing in a choir standing out in the open. When it begins to rain, she registers the drops with a kind of joyous welcome. As the rain gets heavier and her fel-low-singers run for cover, she is left alone, ecstatically singing a single note, with the rain running down her face like blissful tears.

At the centre of each part is the pure and bell-like singing voice of the first Véronique, which continues to dominate the score, the audience and the mind of the second Véronique beyond the death of the first. The role of the voice and its capacity to move is indeed the crux of the film. The film's titles are prefaced by two brief scenes, one in Poland, one in France, in which a mother's quiet voice is heard as she speaks to her little girl. The first little girl, who is destined to die, is encouraged to look at the night stars and the Milky Way, her head upside down; the second little girl, who will survive the first, is shown a leaf in spring sunshine, her head the right way up. Such an experience leaves a *jouissance* effect of the voice that first caused desire. Poignantly, one can later recognize this mother's voice as that of Irene Jacob, who plays both daughters.

The film exerts a powerful force on the spectator by prob-ing into the question of what Woman is. Such a quest opens out onto matters of desire and *jouissance*, bonding agents be-tween actors and spectators. *Jouissance* effects are libidinal effects caused by subjects trying to regain or maintain a nar-cissistic wholeness and consistency: each woman tries to cre-ate through music a feeling of spiritual and affective oneness with something beyond the experience of everyday life. In Lacan's rethinking of Freud the voice is one of the primordial *objets a*, a left-over residue constituted by the effect of lack and loss on being and body, a structuring force from the Other or outside world, capable of producing material effects.[4] The voice can evoke the feeling of union, oneness and symbiosis by its presence, while its faltering or stopping can produce effects of division, discontinuity or even sheer panic. Indeed, the Other's voice begins to structure the infant through the discourse of the parents as a desiring creature even before it is born. As infant it begins to build a relation between voice – words and sounds – and the libidinal effects that the voice produces in its body. The voice and gaze are both first incorporated by the infant as partial drives in concrete response to the mother's voice and look. The result is a locating of the infant as a subject of desire in the Other, in the field of the social. From then on, the scopic drive (associated with the eye) essentially involves the subject's constitution of itself in relation to others: 'what is involved in the drive is "making oneself seen" (*se faire voir*). The activity of the drive is concentrated in this "making oneself" (*se faire*); by the same token the activity involved in the invocatory drive is "making oneself heard" '.[5] Wanting to be seen and heard is to demand the narcissistic reassurance of being recognized. Thus, in the invocatory fantasy the subject exists in relation to an imaginary voice, which does not imply that the voice is imaginary. Rather, fantasy has the power to produce effects in the body, including the 'sense' that the voice itself possesses a specific knowledge.

The voice in the film functions as an *objet a:* one of Lacan's definitions of the *objet a* is the semblance that is taken to fill the void left by the loss of the maternal Thing, a loss which elicits desire for ever after. In the film the voice as *objet a* forms a trap for narcissism, confirming the identity of the first Véronique, the Polish Veronika, and by implication, that of the spectator captivated by her singing and the musical score. When Veronika enters an important singing competition, she is supremely confident about her voice, and she wins, oblivious to the chagrin of another competitor. However, the moment when in the midst of a concert performance her voice falters and the music stops is precisely when her *jouissance* returns directly in her body in the form of a cardiac symptom; the real, the order of the unconscious trauma, ruptures the apparent cohesion of the symbolic.

Premonitions of this possibility are sounded earlier and are poetically caught by the camera, first in a breakdown of geometral seeing. A shot of a Polish landscape is taken from a stationary position, until the landscape begins to move, indicated by a shift of almost imperceptible vertical distorting flaws in what turns out to be the window of a slow-moving train. The objects in the landscape wriggle and twist; there could hardly be a more effective metaphor of the uncanny, anamorphic disturbance of the gaze of the Other. Veronika is then shown sitting in the railway carriage compartment by the window, uncannily doubled by the reflection. Her self-absorbed look is caught as she gazes into the camera, followed by her playful attempt to refract the world outside in a glass ball which is flecked with stars, recalling the night stars and the mother's voice. The landscape goes the opposite way, as if backwards in time, trying to recover what is lost.

In each case the first Véronique's tenuous hold on the symbolic is imaged by the faltering of representation. Most clearly ominous is the slanting of the landscape in a premonitory heart attack: she supports herself on a wall covered with dead leaves, the silhouette of a graveyard in the background, then runs to a park bench and slumps sideways. Her oblique view of the landscape is captured by the camera, tilting the fragility of the geometral space we normally take for granted: momentarily the world is out of joint, just as in the previous sequence shot from the train window. At this very moment her upside-down world is harshly invaded by the mark of sexual difference, the flash of a penis from a passing male exhibitionist. The scene ends as she takes out a stick of lipsalve, restoring her face, with an absent-mindedness that sharpens the irony of the phallic significance of her action. In Part 2 the lipsalve turns up again in her double's handbag, but is there not given a phallic signification. A lipsalve is sometimes just a lipsalve. In the second case it is no more than a poetic link to the double.

These signs do not enter the consciousness of the first Véronique. Even the sight of her French double, on a visit to Poland, getting on a coach some distance away and pointing a camera in her direction, is only half registered by her. Yet here the mirror-image, her twin, is invading the space of the look, uncannily undermining the familiar identification by being too familiar, subjectively disturbing the place where the subject is accustomed to take itself as an object. For an instant she fleetingly sees herself seeing herself. But this Véronique is immune to all omens, so intensely does she live in the moment. In another incident, while visiting a much-loved aunt, she describes, giggling somewhat uneasily, her union with her lover in the rain. But at that moment the aunt, after initially encouraging her niece to speak, abruptly breaks off the talk – which included references to death by heart attack— in order to speak to her lawyer concerning the making of her will, a further reminder of death. Here Veronika is brought up short by the arrival of the symbolic (law), reduced to a lawyer who is a dwarf, fleetingly glimpsed. This, disturbingly, leaves the aunt all the more powerful, a profoundly ambiguous figure: as maternal superego, she towers over the male dwarf and the gentle fathers of the two women.

Veronika's composure is undisturbed to the end. The fatal moment – her collapse while singing in a choral concert – is a shock for the concert and cinema audience, but not for her, since she does not heed the ominous faltering and flattening of her bell-like voice as it loses pitch and almost runs down, introducing the discontinuity that betrays automatism when she is at the height of her *jouissance*. Music here and elsewhere in the film provides an intimation of a *jouissance*, supplementary to the phallic, of which, according to Lacan, woman partakes, though she does not know it.[6] There is a short sequence when Veronika and an older woman are singing a duet during which they acknowledge their mutual enjoyment to each other. Subsequently this woman rejoins the chorus while Veronika remains alone, just as she did at the beginning of the film when the rest of the choir fled from the rain. At this instant of imaginary unity, she collapses and dies of a heart attack. The end of this sequence gives a glimpse of her funeral, with a shot taken from the position of the corpse; gravel is thrown by the mourners slowly covering the screen, thus blacking out the spectator along with the victim, as if to figure Veronika's collapse as a kind of psychotic blackout.

The second Véronique plays out the subjectivity of woman in a different mode, acting with a halting sensitivity. She lives alone in an apartment, works as a teacher, visits her father to speak of her life, but also of his. This father exercises his paternal function, speaking of her mother as one who has sustained his desire all his life. This Véronique is also momentarily ravaged by *jouissance*: while with her first lover, a fellow-teacher, she hears the singing voice of her double whose death she divines – another coinciding of love and death. The next scene shows her giving up her singing lessons, quite unable to account for this decision, from then on devoting herself wholly to her work as a music teacher.

Unlike the first Véronique, this woman embodies the enigma of hysteria such that her lack is all at the surface. That is to say, the loss with which the hysteric identifies manifests itself in the second Véronique in palpable symptoms of uncertainty: her tentativeness, her wish to please others, her unsure apprehension of a ground for being. Unlike her counterpart, she learns to read the ruptures of the symbolic. She knows her frailty and her proximity to the real of death; aware of her heart condition, she accepts treatment.

Her second lover is a writer and a puppeteer. The relationship begins at her school where she watches a puppet show of his in which a girl ballerina collapses in death and is resurrected (to the sound of the first Véronique's singing voice). He succeeds in provoking Véronique's desire, catching sight of her in a mirror at the very moment that he magisterially transforms the dead figure of the puppet into a butterfly-angel. He subsequently brings Véronique to him through providing a series of enigmatic clues (a phonecall of noises, a shoelace, and recorded sounds on a cassette). He thus further provokes her desire, symbolically 'calling' her to him by making her decode the messages. On meeting him she is at first disappointed because he tells her he only wanted to know 'if it were possible that a woman would respond to the call of a stranger'. She runs from him in panic, fearing that he has not chosen her after all and only wants her for her capacity to be manipulated like a puppet. Later, her sadness is palpable when he draws her attention to 'her' photograph, but it is in fact that of her double, taken by her unknowingly on her visit to Poland. Her lover's efforts to console her culminate in their sexual union, the act punctuated by her birdlike cries of sexual joy, as if beyond herself, on the boundaries of the real, rather than in the imaginary, as with the first couple's union in the rain.

The puppeteer makes two female puppets in her likeness, a gesture which refers back to the director's own aesthetic act in creating two Véroniques. Watched by Véronique, the puppeteer stages the uncanny life of one of them through his deft manipulation of its rods while its twin lies inert below. 'Why two?', she asks. 'I need more than one, they get damaged', he replies. The movement of the rods causes anxious painful little sounds which are reminiscent of the cries made by Véronique during the act of love. The experiments of the puppeteer can be seen as an engagement with subjectivity in general: he divines and indeed partakes of the fragility of the feminine, wanting the woman to participate in his exploration (just as he did when he 'called' her to him). Continuing in the self-referential mode, he tells her the story of the two puppets: 'I think I'll call it "The Double Life of . . . " I haven't decided what names to give them'. This could be where the film ends but it is not the final scene. At this point she goes out without a word, precisely because the puppeteer is not quite able to confirm her in her destiny, her place in the Other. The history of the family is more crucial to women than men, because the symbolic is more homely (*heimlich*) to men than to women. Indeed, the final scene shows Véronique revisiting the parental home and being welcomed by the father.

Clearly Kieslowski is as fascinated with the question of what Woman wants as were Freud and Lacan. Via the centrality of the voice and Woman as its embodiment he looks for a way to close the void left by the loss of the primal object, showing that Woman herself is an enigma that man tries to pin down, both directly in relationships and via the substitution of his work. The director here works with his perplexity about Woman by focusing on the voice as an object that causes desire. He keeps out of the film the primal object, the mother, missing from the life of each Véronique, and substitutes the voice as lost object. The 'illness' in the woman – the 'heart' disease – can also stand as the paradigmatic condition of human subjectivity *per se*. Zbigniew Preisner's haunting score weaving through the film invokes that excess of pleasure/pain which signals an illusory lost plenitude which for the man gives rise to the fantasy of woman as a guarantor of his phallic potency, and for the woman continues and preserves her link with the primary object, the maternal body, the Thing. In showing the first Véronique as deriving bliss from the vocal and auditory, the director represents the woman's relation to desire as a relation to the real of the (mother's) body and hence subject to the death drive, a piece of life retained and relived as inert. The death drive emerges where the demands of culture for repression and renunciation are undermined by a drive for the pleasure of oneness associated with the lost object. The result is a repetition of those experiences which lead to *jouissance* effects that gather around loss in the attempt to regain consistency. In each case there is an unconscious fantasy: for man, woman is a symptom of his ontological consistency, she is 'all' to him; for woman, man is 'not all' – the 'heart' disease preserves her existence on the boundaries of the symbolic, closer to the Thing than her male counterpart.

The film poses the question about woman's existence in two different modes. The first Véronique's hysteria takes the form of closing off lack and living in the precarious plenitude of the moment: the second Véronique is a true hysteric, speaking her lack through her body, knowing there is no plenitude. Both women express the unhappy truth of the sexual relation: there is a sexual act (crucial in both parts of the film) but its *jouissance* is dependent on unconscious fantasy. And fantasy creates disharmony or difference, not the oneness of two. Anxiety, doubt and questions intrude: for the first Véronique there is the alienating encounter with the aunt; for the second, the intense experience of loss as she divines her double's death. The first woman burns herself out in persistent repeated ecstasies, in too great an expenditure of *jouissance*, a symptom of too close an identification with the lost mother. In consequence she is unable to define herself adequately in the symbolic. Her excess is not tamed, except by death. The second woman lives in ontological uncertainty: she shrinks from demonstrative ecstasy and lives out her loss by surrendering her singing voice and moderating her *jouissance* into tenderness for father and lover. Although she too is shaken by the call of *jouissance* through the intimation of her double's death, she is able to renounce a part of it to live with others. Each woman exists precariously, constantly challenged by the man's unconscious demand that she be all to him, when she cannot, being herself subject to loss. The question of how woman exists, what she wants, is left hanging in the unspoken answer of the death of the first and the unspoken question of the continuing life of the second.

The intriguing problematic that defines the movement of the story is the director's desire to know how similar women can be so different one from the other. He tries to elicit the difference between them by attributing identical physical properties to two different modes of desire. In posing rather than answering the question of what a woman wants, the director is giving desire the dominant position, above knowledge, as in the discourse of the analyst. He thereby positions the spectator as split subject, uncertain where to place itself in relation to desire. He allows precedence to the poetics of the text as generated by its cinematic discourse, suspending his mastery to allow the spectator to do some of the work of analysis.

Part III

Patients and Analysts: Readers and Texts

9

What is a clinical 'case'?

A clinical case – in the sense of a case report – is a verbal or written account of the treatment of a suffering person; being an account, it is no different from anything else that is open to a range of interpretations. Therefore, a clinical case, like a literary or any other text, cannot provide a clear-cut answer to the question of what it is. Like a director/author, the analyst/therapist must leave a space for further interpretation when presenting his or her case to others.

Rival interpretations

Recent comparative versions of clinical commentaries on cases, published in the *British Journal of Psychotherapy*, have documented responses to the same clinical material made by clinicians of different schools. I propose to take up one such case, which originated in the USA, and was commented upon by two American clinicians as part of a conference held in Chicago in 1995, and later by a British clinician.[1] After the original case presentation, issues arose concerning how to understand the session in terms of a number of factors: various theoretical models, techniques, resonances from a supervisor, suitability of the patient for analysis, integration of theory and practice, and interventions at certain critical moments. I have selected portions of the case presentation to make a brief comparison between the three commentators on the case.

Case Presentation: The Social Construction of Analytic Space

The presenter's theoretical orientation is not specified, other than that he is an American professor of psychology and an advanced candidate in psychoanalytic training. The case concerns an analysis of three years with a man 'who deeply wanted to have [analysis] but almost as deeply could not bring himself to have one' (p. 364). The clinician raises two problems at the outset, first, the difficulty of condensing an analysis of three years into a few pages, and second, that of the successful management of an analysis with someone who was so ambivalent about it. The patient was forty-one, gay, single, employed in the public sector, 'a tall athletic-looking, handsome man who appeared his age' and who always brought a leather gym bag-cum-briefcase with him which he set down by the couch and held on to (p. 364). The *New York Times* would stick out of the pocket and the patient would make reference to anything in the paper concerning gay matters, psychology or child abuse. The analyst found his selections 'interesting' and 'evocative'. In the first session the patient referred to a gay newspaper, and the analyst asked him whether he was trying to let him know he was gay. The patient was startled, wondering if this was an obstacle to analysis and was relieved to find that it was not. The analyst again noted his own liking for the patient whom he found 'very appealing', 'someone who threw out tantalising titbits to engage me' (p. 365). The patient, who knew he was very bright, was ashamed of what he felt to be his underachievements in life, both on a personal and professional level. When he was two years old, his parents divorced and his father's business failed. From then on the family consisted of the mother, the maternal grandmother, and two sisters; within the family the patient was considered too feminine. The divorce was kept secret from the children, and the father's absence and annual visits were explained by the distant location of his work. Often these visits did not happen and the patient suffered the pain of longing, of waiting for a father that never appeared. His grandmother killed herself when the patient was seven and it was he who found her dead. The patient received a good education and subsequently attended medical school, but left after one semester owing to feelings of anxiety and panic arising out of his first homosexual relationships. He saw a therapist over five years and eventually went to work in Europe at the age of twenty-six. After eight years he returned to the USA but was too ashamed to recontact his therapist.

In the early days of his new analytic treatment he expressed the hope that the analysis would get him back into medical school. He continued to complain about what he called his 'projection problems' (thinking, for instance, that the session was in some way bugged and transmitted to his mother) which the analyst saw as fantasies of a psychotic type. His first dream was as follows:

> P: I was in Istanbul again on vacation— a horrible scene of animals being mistreated. After I buy something in the market, an ugly hooker offers to pay but I politely decline. I travel with her in a bus that stops at the sea. Men are tearing the animals' innards out – incredible cruelty to the animals. (p. 367)

The patient was then asked for his associations:

> P: Exposure, abuse, desire to make myself shameful.
>
> A: Perhaps the dream has to do with starting analysis.
>
> P: I guess that's the case. In a thorough analysis you come out completely different. In the dream you're grasping, condescending, indifferent and manipulative – possibly vicious.
>
> A: Who am I?
>
> P: The hooker. I can't decide if she's sweet, pitiable or manipulative. I felt idyllic waiting for the appointment outside the office today. I only felt that way at my (paternal) grandparents'. I can hear my own ambivalence. I worry you're a jerk. My reason tells me there's no reason to feel that way.
>
> A: You're having a hard time deciding whether it's an idyllic world here or Istanbul.
>
> P: The indifference of the animal handlers – and a dog was eating animal innards – was horrible and then waiting outside

here was so beautiful. You might do to me what was being done to those animals. My motto in Latin would be 'Trust no one'.

The patient, whose appointments were early in the morning four times a week, soon started to miss sessions without notice or comment. He said he wanted to spare his analyst some unpleasant projection and did not feel under any obligation to give notice, since he was paying and there was no personal relationship. Soon there were long silences within the sessions he did attend. The analyst said, 'I'm thinking that some feeling of anger plays a part here in the silent treatment'.

I asked him when he did such things as ending the session himself or taking the tissue for his head with him (so that he wouldn't be beholden to me for cleaning up after him), if it mattered how I experienced it?

P: I don't think you would tell me.

A: Suppose I did?

P: Until you do, it's hypothetical.

I thought that I needed to say something or a series of things to try and get through to him, not to participate in his working model that has us so unrelated. I said:

A: Well, I find it somewhat provocative and annoying. So what does that factor into the equation for you?

Mr. L was not convinced. He said:

P: Well, I'm not sure you do. You may just be saying it as a heuristic device.

I told Mr. L that his comment was very dismissive of me. He replied:

P: There's no reason to think that everything you're saying isn't a calculated attempt to make me angry.

With that he ended the session a few minutes early (so that I wouldn't be 'kicking him out'), picked up his tissue, smiled and left.

I thought that the fact of his re-engaging the dialogue with me and smiling as he left suggested that while he wouldn't overtly acknowledge what I said, some of it was getting through. (p. 368)

The analyst and patient continued in a piecemeal fashion. They eventually examined the patient's endless waiting for the father that never came, and how this was repeated in the treatment in silences and missed sessions. The analyst imparted more of his feelings, saying that he felt 'denigrated, treated like a robot, like nothing', and that the patient was 'behaving just as he described his abusive family'. The analyst added that he 'wasn't quite sure about any of it', and needed his patient to say more (p. 369). There were more silences and absences, until eventually the patient expressed appreciation of his analyst's staying involved with him. Finally the patient re-entered medical school, despite his analyst's misgivings. The analyst concluded his account by saying that he believed 'a detailed attention to the social aspects of the relationship was crucial in making this analysis operative and in creating a useful context for examining and analysing the patient's troubled and conflictual unconscious' (p. 370).

Commentary from the self psychology point of view

The commentator expresses appreciation of the difficult nature of a case where the patient does not speak or attend his sessions. She recognizes that changes have been achieved, but sees them as having come about as the result of a 'corrective [. . .] emotional experience' rather than that of 'the interpretation of the mutually constructed analytic relationship'. With the original clinician the commentator locates the source of the patient's attitude and behaviour in his father's neglect of him, since the patient's 'temporary withdrawal must have seemed the only way he could regulate the repetition of his childhood trauma'. Nevertheless, the patient was able on a pre-conscious level to appreciate the attempts of his analyst to help him. When his analyst reached the point of translating the patient's thoughts, a 'merger transference' began to form, an attempt to fuse with the analyst, which, according to the commentator, supported the patient's sense of self, and at the same time enabled him to find a benevolent father-figure, thus helping him to exchange his old secretiveness for a new openness. Although, as a result, the transference took on an idealizing form, with a 'primitive form of grandiosity' in place of his schizoid defences, it turned into a 'healthy enactment' (p. 371). The patient responded to the analyst's active efforts to engage with him by idealizing the relationship to the point of attributing omnipotence to him, but over time was able to transform his idealizing transference into a trust that allowed him to act more autonomously. Where the commentator differed from the original analyst was in attributing the success of the treatment to the social aspects of the relationship, seeing it rather as turning a fragmenting experience into a 'primitive merger experience' and 'corrective (selfobject) emotional experience' (p. 372), that is, together with his analyst the patient was able to build up a new measure of internal certainty. The commentator concludes by stating her belief that the character of the therapist counts as much as technique or theoretical stance.

Commentary from the object-relations point of view

The commentator points to the conflictual nature of the patient's entry into analysis, wanting it and not wanting it. The patient was 'shame-prone', like his parents who hid their divorce as if it were a defect under a pretence of marriage. The commentator points to the patient's fear of the analyst as displayed in the 'ugly hooker' dream and sees it as a symptom of his sense of inadequacy, of his shame and fear about the defects that might be revealed in the course of the treatment: 'Mr L's pained response to an imperfectly attuned analytic intervention forces him into awareness of his need for the analyst's understanding and the shame of this experience is

unbearable' (p. 372); that is to say, when he does not feel perfectly understood, he believes that the analyst is malevolently
disposed towards him just as he thinks his family were. The
commentator locates the patient's shame in his fruitless wait
for the father whom he wanted but who did not want him.
Moreover, the death of his grandmother, discovered by him,
confirmed his view that 'his needs can drive others to destruction' (p. 373). The transference is thus a double trap for the
patient: he is fulfilling a need that is shameful and dangerous
for him to acknowledge, and he is also fearful of destroying
his object. This leads him to seek 'a relationship without affective content', to miss sessions and to refuse to speak (p.
373). 'The anxiety of others seeing his defect is at the root of
his paranoia', and the 'nasty projections' from which he suffers refer to 'his experience of others when they see inside
him' (p. 372). When the patient tells his analyst that waiting
outside his room is 'beautiful', this testifies to the patient's
wish to be near but not too near, a fear of 'object contact', this
being the fundamental dynamic of the schizoid position as
described by W. Ronald Fairbairn (p. 373). The commentator,
alluding also to D. W. Winnicott, argues that the analysis must
meet an early need, where dependency is not experienced as
shameful. He expresses doubt that the analyst's disclosure of
his feelings (the so-called countertransference response) was
helpful; on the contrary, the patient might think that the analyst's agenda was being unloaded upon him, which repeats his
interchange with his parents, thus causing him to respond with
more silence. 'The analyst's "getting through" is [the patient's]
submission once again to the other's agenda' (p. 374). The
commentator suggests another approach, that of addressing
the patient's fear of emotional contact by, for example, com-
menting on his need to hold onto his gym bag as evidence of
his mistrust. Although this commentator would not interfere
with the patient's silence, he would interpret it to him as his
being able to continue in analysis only by creating as much
distance as possible: 'I would not use as a criterion for intervention my own need to analyse because this need of mine
would not fit the patient's need', but would rather 'participate in the patient's silence' (p. 375).

Comments by a post-Kleinian psychotherapist

The commentator wants his account to be regarded as provisional because he feels the lack of sessional material. He also questions the criteria for success and the claim that the analytic space was 'socially constructed'. He wonders whether this claim refers to his re-entry into medical school or to 'the patient's growing adaptive capacities in the transference' (p. 376). He also comments on the lack of material to do with three elements, the infantile, the sexual and the 'emotional linking'. As regards the first, the infantile, the commentator sees the dialogue between patient and analyst as always between one adult and another, and he wants to know how the analyst experiences his patient's infantile life, as, for example, what the father is doing while he is away, who is with him, why it is not his son. As regards the second, the sexual, he notes that the patient brings homosexuality via the *New York Times* and that 'the analyst obviously finds the patient both attractive and seductive' (p. 376). When the analyst interprets to the patient that he wishes to reveal that he is gay, the commentator asks whether there could not 'also have been a wish, a question, about the analyst's sexuality' (p. 377). In the Istanbul dream it may not only be the analyst who is the hooker but also the paying patient. The commentator points out that the patient's breakdown at medical school was connected with his emerging sexuality, yet there is no mention of the analyst's experience of any sexual transference: 'I shouldn't be surprised if, in the present-day USA, it would be the extreme of political incorrectness to interpret homosexual matters: but I have a sense of a much more unconscious avoidance' (p. 377) which suggests an unexamined countertransference on the part of the analyst. As regards the third element, emotional linking, the commentator refers to a lack of curiosity in the patient that borders on the pathological, a 'massive exercise in -K' (Bion's symbol for the infant's rejection of knowledge, which leads to meaningless experience and feelings of internal terror): 'such emotionally loaded events as the parental separation, grandmother's suicide, father's not turning up', (p. 377) were presented but not analysed in terms of the unconscious meaning that the patient assigned to them. The patient's confusion of role – parent/child, man/woman, hooker/client – was likewise never examined; neither was the psychic significance of his return to medical school. The part that anger played in the transferential relationship was also left unclear. Moreover, the commentator feels that the analyst's disclosure of his own thoughts to the patient rather than his staying with the patient's attitude towards him had an effect of muddying the waters: 'the analyst says "Fortunately or unfortunately, as we reviewed his history, the transference manifestations were very strong". That unfortunately bears a great deal of examination' (p. 377). In sum, the commentator believes that what has not been detected in this case is an unconscious fantasy of a destructive parental union ending in mutilation, death and the destruction of children at birth. Therefore, 'to assign meanings to what the patient brings to analysis would be to bring the dead to life and thus to have to confront the monsters', something 'too dreadful to contemplate' (p. 377).

These commentaries, coming from a variety of theoretical orientations which emerge clearly in the stance adopted, illustrate the constant possibility that the focus of interpretation can widen as well as contract. For there is not one discrete element to be selected and seen from different viewpoints, but, rather, it is the different points of view, that can omit or select from a given context what is to constitute the focus of interpretation. Interpretations change according to the context that is presumed to be relevant, just as the significance of a poetic image will change according to the frame that is put around it. By the same token the content of a clinical symptom is not a rigid element but a formal envelope containing different messages in different contexts: what determines the relevance in every case is desire, both conscious and unconscious, of all those involved in the situation. This indeed is implicit in the Introduction to the above commentaries, which goes under the rubric of 'Contemporary ways of hearing: Multiple models in psychoanalytic treatment'; it

ends with a brief questionnaire dealing with diagnostic understanding on the level of symptom and relationship,
theoretical orientation, technique and strategy, effect of supervision, analytic suitability of patient, relation of theory to
practice, and moments of crisis – all of which involves subjective data.

Returning to the original case presentation, with its emphasis on the 'social construction of analytic space', we might
detect a shortfall of the poetic which has repercussions on
the clinical effect. The clinician exercises an intersubjective
competence, with undoubted beneficial consequences for the
patient's current life, but, since most of the work is done at a
pre-conscious level, the longer-term effects of the treatment
are left as a question in the clinician's mind. The theoretical
and practical reluctance to operate at an unconscious level
shows itself in his limited ability to work with the reversibil-
ity of meaning, what we might call a poetic deficiency. The
post-Kleinian commentator picks up some instances which
illustrate this point: the analyst sees the patient's concern
with his homosexuality but not his curiosity regarding the
analyst's sexuality. Hence he does not pick up the possibility
that the 'hooker' might be both himself *and* the patient, which
then leads to a conflation of role as to whose anger is at stake.
The post-Kleinian commentator is nearest to the classical
Freudian (and also to the Lacanian) in this array, since he
looks for the fundamental fantasy which props up the patient's identifications but which is at the same time a horror
to him and perhaps also to his analyst. This fantasy is best
tapped at the level of the patient's words ('men are tearing
animals' innards out – incredible cruelty to the animals') than
at the level of emotions (who is angry with whom), since
countertransference is essentially unconscious. It is interesting that the most admiring commentary on the case comes
from a self psychologist, who, like the original analyst, also
works at the level of the ego and regards the analyst's sharing
of his and the patient's feelings as a 'healthy enactment',
amounting to a 'corrective (selfobject) emotional experience',
the analyst making up for the father's neglect by offering
himself to the patient as a better father-figure. But, although

such communication may have a therapeutic effect in bringing about some change, it is not clear whether this change will extend beyond the symptom, a doubt also implicit in the commentary of the post-Kleinian therapist. The therapy seems rather an attempt to reach an imaginary endpoint, an impossible coincidence of understanding which would serve to erase the poetic potential of the analytic process. Indeed, the self psychologist betrays a misconception about the unconscious in speaking of the patient's 'secretiveness', for the unconscious is precisely not what the patient is 'secretive' about since he is not in full possession of his secret. The object-relations commentator, on the other hand, like the post-Kleinian, is alert for concealed meanings and open to the ambivalence of objects, be they dreams, kit bags, waiting rooms or silences.

The question of evidence

These comparisons once again raise the questions of what scientific status to give these rivalries of theory and practice, and what purpose such comparisons serve. To what extent is it even possible to rely on material which is largely in summary form? In his book *The Rhetorical Voice of Psychoanalysis* (1994) Donald Spence[2] argues as follows: as psychoanalysis has advanced, flaws in the presentation of case material have arisen through reducing the amount of original material included, for the absence of actual statements made by analyst and analysand prevents an analytic audience from searching out ambiguities and producing alternative readings. Case studies now tend towards summaries and the paraphrasing of material, with selected anecdotal evidence (the famous clinical 'vignette') already slanted towards a particular theory. As a result, hypotheses get treated as facts. The tendency is to tell a single story, to present dubious guesses as knowable realities, and to assume the mantle of authority, particularly by appealing to past authority. This apparently unexceptionable argument leads Spence to demand that the strict empirical criteria adopted by modern natural science ought also to be applied to psychoanalysis: it should be possible to have free discussion of reproducible evidence together with full awareness that the presented facts are theory-laden. When looking at case material there should be open disagreement so that 'an uncompelled consensus' (Jürgen Habermas)[3] can be arrived at as a result of dialogue. Spence goes so far as to claim that psychoanalysis, if it does not supply verbatim case material, elevates itself to a false authority not far removed from that of alchemy. As an example, Spence cites a case where he believes an analyst has concluded on very slender evidence that an actual homosexual seduction has taken place in the patient's past, whereas it could be a manifestation of transference within the session. Spence takes this as a proof that replicable public data are required.

One can agree that Spence's example shows that interpretations can be distorted by countertransference (as the post-Kleinian showed for a similar situation above). However, this argument misses his ideal of scientific objectivity because the very recording of analytic material has an effect on what transpires in the session so that the 'replicable public data' is contaminated from the outset. If, as in the commentaries just considered, a comparison is made between readings of the same case, it is possible to discriminate between rival interpretations grounded in different theories without having precise replicable data.

In order to get the kind of evidence comparable with that of the 'hard' sciences, neurophysiological evidence would be required, which might in the distant future possibly provide support for psychoanalysis. Lacan began by distinguishing between the 'exact sciences' (to do with presumed objects) and the 'conjectural sciences' (concerned with subjects operating in the symbolic) but argued that the distinction was not absolute.[4] He thought of psychoanalysis as conjectural, closer to a discipline like linguistics. Freud himself, though he tried to claim a natural science place for psychoanalysis, nevertheless changed the meaning of biological terms when he employed them (for example 'drive', not just as a biological impulse but as what underlies all purpose and all desire), and thus moved in the 'conjectural' direction. Freud's positivism (or 'scientism', as Lacan called it) has two aspects: an onto-logical one (following the Brücke-Helmholtz school) and an epistemological or methodological one. It can only aspire to the status of science in the first sense, but it can be scientific in the second.

Is psychoanalysis a science? From the sixteenth century onwards science took itself to be in search of facts already given, defining itself in relation to its objects. Freud, without actually addressing the question of the philosophy of science, always kept a foot in both camps, never giving up the notion of the drive as the source of all human action and at the same time wrestling with the discontents of civilization, the lot of the psyche within culture. Lacan too saw the human being from the beginning as exiled from nature but he did not wish to make an absolute opposition between the exact sciences and the conjectural sciences. Unlike Carl Jung, who thought in terms of the collective unconscious, defining the uncon-scious as being structured by archetypal images, Lacan defines the unconscious as structured like a language, seeing language as constitutive of the subject from its inception, and therefore suggesting that the solution to the theory of knowledge and the place of science in it lies in pursuing the relation of lan-guage to the world. If the subject that is making the scientific judgements is itself involved in the process of the scientific definition of objects then exactitude emerges as a regulative idea (Kant), something that is imposed by subjects as a neces-sary guide in the world.

Lacan considers that the epistemological trajectory must move from the object of science, as historically conceived from Galileo through to Karl Popper, to the 'subject of science'. Instead of beginning with a commonsense world in which sci-ence is defining ever more exactly a pre-existing set of entities and properties, to arrive at truth one must analyse the 'one' that is observing, the subject itself. Lacan detects in the key philosopher of the scientific revolution, René Descartes him-self, a move that betrays an implicit recognition of this: in Descartes' own epistemological method, the fundamental re-jection of all knowledge, Lacan perceives an unwitting admis-sion of the 'emptiness of the subject'. After this sceptical reduction which amounts to the evacuation of all contents of knowledge, we are left with the punctiliar 'I' of the 'I think' which itself has no content and is, as it were, a vanishing point. Descartes' admission of the emptiness of the subject was unwitting since in fact he did not recognize the subject as empty but, paradoxically, as full: he fills the void of the subject with *res cogitans*, thinking stuff, an entirely imaginary construct, the self as object. Descartes thus forecloses the subject as does modern science that is founded on the *cogito*.

When Descartes proposed his *cogito, ergo sum* '(I think, therefore I am'), he believed that he had arrived at the one foundational certainty of all knowledge, having rejected all other knowledge as uncertain; but he was thereby revealing that the inhabiting of the personal pronoun is what enables a subject of knowledge to emerge in the first place – its principle of constitution. In itself the 'I' contains no certain knowledge whatsoever, being merely one of the instruments by which, in dialogue with other subjects so constituted, knowledge of all kinds, scientific and quotidian, can be obtained. Lacan makes an analogy between Descartes' 'rejection of all knowledge' and the 'foreclosure' of the psychotic, who, because of the problematic nature of his relation to language, is unable to begin the process that will make him into a subject, thus arguing that Cartesian science and psychosis have the same structure. It is language that provides the human being with that which enables it to become a subject, namely, with the empty unity of the personal pronoun, 'I'. In both the discourse of Cartesian science and that of the psychotic, the subject is foreclosed and the self becomes an object: the psychotic cannot become a subject because he or she does not inhabit language but is inhabited by it.

Admitting the unconscious into science implies that scientific progress cannot be an ordered succession of 'conjectures and refutations' in the Popperian manner. Lacan, with Gaston Bachelard, regards it as delusional to imagine that each progressive step lies within the logic of the theoretical order of received opinion.[5] For Lacan scientific knowledge has to be culled directly from the real, thereby upsetting the existing paradigms, invading the old terms, with which it proves itself 'incommensurable': a new hypothesis comes about from a new interpretation derived from encountering the real, not from a reordering of already existing entities. Science is thus responsible for the creation-by-selection of the objects it produces. This is why Lacan invented the neologism *operçevoir*, a portmanteau word running together *opérer* ('to operate') and *perçevoir* ('to perceive') [6] – both what the eye and ear 'half create, and what perceive' (Wordsworth).[7] Thus for Lacan language operates deceptively to produce both subjects and objects out of the real, 'deceptively' because the word can never wholly capture the real, in every case leaving an unconscious remainder wherein lies the truth of the subject, its *jouissance* .

Therefore, within the scientific world of psychoanalysis, the analyst is not an impartial observer but must be included within the 'clinical fact'. Even where video- or audio-taped recordings are available, to bring them in is to alter the analysis. In the analyst's presentation of a case history, his or her 'story' of the sessions, selection is unavoidable and will be influenced by a variety of factors (the occasion of the presentation, the speaker's professional standing, the emotional response of the patient/reader, etc.) just as is the case with any storyteller. There is no ideal situation where no interpretation is involved.[8] Of course there is no harm in trying to objectify the subjective at the therapeutic level, to arrive at understandable empirical evidence, but any method which involves the unconscious will have to deal with tropes, puns and ironies; there will be poetics lying in the unconscious evidence and lying in the conscious one. The more we hear the analyst's struggle to understand and the more we can compare rival interpretations, the more we can evaluate how conclusions are drawn. The analyst, like the author, will always say more than he knows. How far is it possible to monitor the affective response of the analyst, his countertransference in Freudian terms, his 'desire' in Lacanian ones? Every analysis is different, which will affect the trajectory of the so-called cure: because analysts are dealing with material of such complexity, there are bound to be differences, both of method and interpretation, and this will apply even where the same theory is held. Clinical events can be linked up in many different ways, providing poetic connections that involve a rhetorical effort to cause a transformation, as shown in the next chapter.

10

The rhetoric of clinical discourse: Dialogue with Sammy

Joyce McDougall's account of an analysis, supervised by Serge Lebovici, of a nine-year-old boy afflicted by a psychotic disorder is unique in providing a verbatim report of a five-times-a-week treatment conducted over eight months.[1] For a considerable time the young patient made a habit of ordering his analyst to write down the stories and dramas he made up, and then to read them back to him. In their ensuing dialogue he very often asked her to reply in writing, with the result that their sometimes almost one-line stichomythic interchange has something of the quality of Greek drama:

S.   You're a funny psychoanalyst!

J.M.   Why is that?

S.   They're usually fierce like this (screws his face up in a grimace). They do that to frighten you. But I like to have a silly psychoanalyst. Do you like Dr Lebovici? I went to see him once. Don't you think he's better than you?

J.M.   You thought he was fierce?

S.   Yes. I'm frightened of him.

J.M.   It's better to have a psychoanalyst who is frightening?

S.   I wonder why I think he is better than you?

J.M.   Because he's a man?

S.   Yes, perhaps. (He taps my chest with a pencil and giggles.)

J.M.   You think you'd be safer with him?

S.   I'm going to work with him. I don't suppose he has any games like this. I'd be bored there. But just for the first few days I'd be frightened. Oh boy! I wish I was the psychoanalyst! You have big trouble.
      (He taps my breasts. I tell him he can talk about my breasts but not hit me . . .) (p. 116)

Here already this case history exhibits the poetics of the unconscious. What is the analytic couple doing together? The patient has an unconscious rhetoric and within the transference situation the analyst brings her conscious rhetoric to bear on his in an effort to allow him to word his anxieties, to make his rhetoric conscious. Although at that time his recurring fantasies are to do with the classical Oedipal conflict, McDougall aptly identifies the more primitive fears still present in the patient's analytical material, such as 'the imago of a devouring mother who wants to take possession of the father's penis and phallic power', which gives rise both to anxious fantasies that the 'castrated' mother/analyst wants to castrate him and to uncertain longings that the powerful father/analyst might protect him. In the above extract Sammy initially locates his fear in the visage of a 'fierce' male analyst, who makes a terrible face to frighten him, and he prefers a 'silly' analyst who seems to be safer.

But then, poetically, what Sammy says is not what he means; like Oedipus, he speaks in an ambiguous language that goes in many directions. Perhaps the fierce father/analyst might be powerful enough to deflect the even bigger threat of the primal object, what Lacan calls 'the Thing'. 'You have big trouble', Sammy says to his analyst – you create a big threat for me. And throughout many sessions Sammy announces the 'trouble' of the day, the particular fantasy that the threat takes; for example, 'Sammy evades the breast-penis anxieties by concentrating solely on behinds'— for instance, the poetry of the 'fart-fart behind' (p. 117).

As can be seen in this example of the analytic couple's dialogue, the analyst tropes her patient's statements in a rhetorical effort to cause a transformation. It is a mutual but asymmetrical dialogue in which, although he tries to render her powerless by insisting she write rather than speak, they are both trying to bring the real – his trauma, his dreaded incestuous wishes (at one point Sammy asks for matches and wants to 'play with fire') – under a more reliable symbolic.

Most of the time the young patient dictates to his analyst in an effort to tell his story, to give his interpretation and not hear hers. A remarkable recurring theme is that of the Magic Face:

> This face is very magic, and that is why it is called the Magic Face. This face can do anything it wants to. If you ever saw it you would be surprised because it can do so many things. For instance it can kill anybody it likes, and make dead people come to life. It could think and talk and everything it wanted before it was born. And the Magic Face can change itself into lions and tigers and hippopotamuses and ants [sic] and uncles. This face is half of everything, half hippo and half tiger, half kangaroo without a second leg, half elephant without a trunk and just like a dog that didn't have no tail and no front paw. So this face is a mongrel just like a dog is a mongrel to other dogs.

> Magic Face can be very frightful sometimes, but once in a while, every Christmas, it makes a smile once in a while, but not all the time. And this face is the magickest face in the world. This face is a big face not a small face. No one ever saw it in the world before. If ever it comes people will be most surprised. Even though it won't really come people can dream about it and think about it as a fairy-tale. (pp. 24–5)

The first paragraph contains a striking parapraxis: why switch from 'aunts' to 'ants'? Why this confusion of categories? The lawful world of kinship and family relations, the symbolic, is here conflated with the jungle of lions and tigers, the real of the drive. The magic face oscillates between a terrifying omnipotence – able both to kill and to awaken the dead – and a frightening authority, the symbolic that was always already there, thinking and talking before Sammy even came onto the scene, bound up with 'everything it [the face] wanted'.[2] This truly Janus-faced image then gets further transformed in an attempt to get out of the impossible confrontation by a turn towards the necessity of castration as a possible, if equally terrifying resolution. A new transformation of the fantasy then proliferates in creatures with missing body parts, and ends up, in an extraordinarily creative turn, with the trope of a trope. To say that the face is a mongrel is equivalent to admitting the polysemic nature of the image: since 'mongrel' is a hybrid of a number of types of dog at once and the face is interpretable on many levels, 'mongrel' becomes a trope of troping. In this meta-psychological understanding the young patient has made an unconscious dialectical advance in understanding his confusion of categories.

A further meta-commentary develops in the second paragraph, where the Magic Face turns into an allegory or fable, 'a fairy-tale'. Sammy is now to some degree conscious that he can use the Magic Face fantasy as an image for his 'trouble', for the disturbance in him. Every Christmas this face, that is also the face of his analyst in the transference, smiles. If it makes a smile, it confirms his dream of omnipotence and becomes the 'magickest face in the world'. For then he himself becomes the power that smiles upon him, 'a big face, not a small face', and everyone will be surprised and will love and admire him. His poetry here makes use of rhyme and assonance, with the rhythmic effect of binding difference with sameness: 'it makes a smile once in a while, but not all the time', with 'face' repeated four times within two lines, leading up to a lyrical crescendo of internal rhyme:

> The place is a face but nobody knows why, but I shall sigh if I know why. HI! said the Face to a tiny little man who only had one hand. But the Face feels sorry for him because he has no chin. Now this man saw a baboon as he was looking at the moon. But now the moon shines low down. As the trees look brown because it's autumn now. How shall I find my way home if the Face doesn't find me? (p. 25)

The face now speaks to him, 'HI!', and feels sorry for him as a being of lack, one who has suffered castration, as if saying 'I am on your side', and thus speaking with him, allowing him a remainder of drive satisfaction – the baboon present within the ideal image of the moon, which is now shining 'low down', yet staying within its sphere. The boundary of time is momentarily appreciated, the trees going brown in autumn, a change of season, perhaps a surrender of the idea of an eternal summer, and an inkling of death. Thus there is a fusion of ideal and real, symbolic and drive, achieved in an imaginary mode in the figure of the face. But then comes the poignant question of the way 'home', addressed to the analyst/(m)Other: How can I be found without you finding me? – in Winnicottian terms, wanting to be found; or, in Lacanian terms, the question of the Other's Desire, what the Other wants of him.

The analytic couple work with these symbolic shifts which produce poetic effects and in which neither of them fully knows what they are saying until it is said, and perhaps not then. The poetic effects occur whenever the symbolic misses the real – poetry takes advantage of this – and at these points the analyst helps her patient to turn threats into stories, using rhythmic devices to redirect desire as it gets stuck in repetition. In the following extract from Sammy's thirty-ninth session he is again troubled by his wandering drive, the source of which is a frightening enigma, prowling and turning 'motionlessly' inside him:

> On the boat there is a little boy called Alex. Alex feeds Wild Horse who turns round motionlessly. He's getting nervous and kicks his stable and is very wild. There's a fire and the boat starts to sink. Night time. Wild Horse kicks to the shore. Alex is with him. Now he's going to train him to be a real tame horse. He kicks and rears and jumps off. (The horse is taken from the scene.) Alex cries, 'Oh, I lost the Wild Horse. I lost him.' He whistles but nothing came. One day he finds him drinking. This horse begins to get tame. Alex rides bareback. 'No, my boy, I'm not going to fall off you! You better be calm.' Wild Horse thought, 'Well, no point in rearing up. I'd better be good.' (pp. 82–3)

The horse 'getting nervous, kicks his stable', his inner stability, his fragile symbolic. The 'horse' (Freud's, and Plato's, image

for the id) gets wild, there is a fire, a disaster, darkness. The
boy Alex struggles to save himself and the wild horse, hoping
to calm the drive, to 'train' the wild horse into a 'real tame
horse'. But for the moment he has to abandon it, 'I lost him';
for a while the symbolic does not get an answer from the real,
'whistles' in vain. Then the drive turns up again, it is drinking,
can be fed, is under his control, and for a while the horse can
be ridden 'bareback', without the restraint of a bridle. The
story continues with a frightening fantasy of the drive once
more getting out of control, the symbolic ('their house') 'starts
to burn', there is a fight, and another horse gets killed by 'Wild
Horse' (p. 83).

But this is nothing compared with the eschatological vision
of a day of judgement as recorded by Sammy's analyst in an
earlier session:

> Soon the oceans of all the world swept over all the land. And
> the earth was covered with water. Ice fell from the sky, the sun
> came out, and the water began to boil. All the animals were in
> dreadful pain. The sun was coming closer. There was fire. Soon
> all was death. Just the earth spinning alone. Everything was
> death. Just the ground burning and the water boiling. The earth
> was getting smaller and smaller till Crash! Bang! Crash! The
> earth hit the sun. And it burst with a tremendous explosion.
> There was not a living thing. What was left of the earth all
> came from the sun. Nothing but ashes. So that was the end of
> the earth.
>
> And now the sun was only with eight planets instead of nine.
> What happened to the world was very sad. Just a little music
> came. Even the Magic Face was dead. It was the only thing
> that could kill her. Then they could see the face in the sky It
> was the Virgin, and her face said, 'Since the earth blew up
> there'll never be another earth ever again.' And that was the
> end of the adventurous planet. The sky got bluer and bluer
> and the Face went away. (pp. 32–3)

Here is a horrifying fantasy of what might happen if the drive
got out of control: the patient is visualizing and voicing his
fear that he will be destroyed by the drive. As the 'adventur-
ous planet', Sammy has been taking too many risks. The result

is that bizarre happenings take place, 'ice fell from the sky', as if this were a version of the Book of Revelation. The earth falls out of orbit and into the sky, an image of the effacement of the subject in the Thing. There is dazzling heat and light, figuring an intensity of unbearable *jouissance*: 'all the animals were in dreadful pain'. Then, 'everything was death', blurred together in one destruction as all boundaries are blotted out, with no distinctions between sea and land, with the earth being covered in water, boiling the creatures on it. The sun (the Thing) now closes in on the helpless earth (himself), which is 'spinning alone', finally bursting 'with a tremendous explosion', destroyed by fire and water: 'so that was the end of the earth'. Along with this disaster, the 'Analyst-Magic Face' (as McDougall calls it, p. 34), is also destroyed in this apocalypse, both rupturing his dream of omnipotence and making him fearful that it is his own omnipotence that has destroyed the object: 'Even the Magic Face was dead. It was the only thing that could kill her'. Yet there is also a poignant vision of a resurrection which excludes the earth (him), since the face, now 'in the sky', pronounces the judgement that 'there'll never be another earth ever again'. Right at the end of this extraordinary narrative and beyond the above text, the sun comes out again and shines on the silence of the void in the universe, 'the empty space' that was once the earth. For Lacan, this moment in the analysis would be one of 'subjective destitution', the draining away of enjoyment (*jouissance*), leaving the subject momentarily bankrupt and without substance.

In her Introduction to this case, McDougall points out that her patient produced the type of fantasies Melanie Klein described as occurring in 'the paranoid-schizoid position'. She then proceeds to elaborate persuasively the treatment of psychotic children from an object-relations point of view and to argue in general for the treatment of these children by psychoanalysis. One could make an equally persuasive case for their treatment from a Lacanian viewpoint, and I have indeed introduced some Lacanian concepts into the discussion. But my brief in this section is not to be partisan, but rather to show the general aesthetic effects produced by symbolic shifts in language in its combination of the literary and the clinical.

Every statement, however ordinary or extraordinary, is a transference of an intensity, which poses new questions that transform what is putatively the same. Meaning derives from the real in each case, partly conscious, partly unconscious. As analysis/life advances, the new information comes from a rereading of the experience, whether literary or clinical. All statements are part-failures, economical truths. Language, the text, 'has organized our disappointment',[3] as we put the symbolic on the real. The analyst will have reflected on his or her practice in learning to read the unconscious. He or she will be aware that both in literary and in clinical discourse neither author nor reader, patient nor analyst, quite knows what they are saying as they are saying it. The statement begins narcissistically and ends by cutting into the imaginary *jouissance* that must be drained from the excess of the demand. For, as can be seen in Sammy's account, the repressed *jouissance* is only too ready to find an illicit outlet in the oppressiveness of the superego.

Although McDougall and Lebovici were on the whole lucky in getting the unconscious of their patient to well up as it did, nevertheless they had to exercise careful clinical management to keep this process going while restraining Sammy from violent behaviour. Initially this young and creatively gifted patient was highly excitable and tried to make a number of assaults on his analyst, attempting to touch her breasts and reach up her skirts, often threatening and once actually hitting her quite violently. He continued with this kind of behaviour intermittently throughout the treatment, testing the analyst's and her supervisor's combined skills in managing the transference as it showed from session to session in the patient's narratives, drawings and play, and in the dialogue in which he and McDougall engaged. To get access to the unconscious in the adult requires a different kind of management, and it is to this challenge that I now turn.

11

The rhetoric of clinical management: Bion and Minuchin

Wilfred Bion

Wilfred Bion, generally regarded as belonging to the pantheon of psychoanalysis, is perhaps best known for his pioneering work with groups and his theories of group behaviour, as well as for his formidably abstract theories on the communicability of unconscious thinking. He is thus most often invoked for his theories and given much credit for his clinical work, but seldom assessed precisely for his clinical contributions. In this section I am principally interested in these contributions as they relate to the management of the psychoanalytic session. For this purpose I have chosen material from his *Clinical Seminars* (1994).[1] The material I am using is drawn from the published recordings that were made in collaboration with his daughter on a visit to Brazil when he was eighty. In the course of this two-week visit he held fifty seminars for a small group of analysts who presented extracts taken from their own practice.

For Bion there is no 'simple' analytic case which might be convenient for the beginner. He encourages his supervisees not to think of their cases as simple: 'I would far rather you had a complicated and horrible supervision than that you had a horrible and complicated analysis' (p. 82). Nevertheless, to

engage the patient into the poetic process of analysis the patient's concepts have to be challenged, so that when the patient says to her analyst 'Why don't you speak to me?', he will
say 'What makes you think I am here to talk to you?' (p. 82).
Immediately the concept of talking is up for a new definition,
as are also her motives for coming.

Bion's response here includes the problems that this patient has had with her refusal to lie down on the couch, the
question of what language was appropriate for the analytic
session, and her unconscious response to being talked about
by her former psychiatrist. To manage all this material, the
analyst has to do more than give interpretations, he 'has to be
an artist – he has to make constructions of what is going on'
(p. 84). Thus he might think that 'to take up these sexual
elements', as the patient does when she talks about her psychiatrist, 'is itself a sexual act, because the situation is one in
which there are two people, in private, talking and using words
like "breast" and "penis"' (p. 84). Patient and analyst are thus
liable to being viewed as behaving in a sexual manner (as if
acting out a primal scene). So there is a double bind: either
the analyst can be accused of not doing analysis (if he keeps
out sexual material), or of talking about sex with a married
woman. Here there is a problem of interpretation, the problem of 'speaking desires can be dangerous'.

Interpretation is always problematized in Bion's seminars,
and may be put thus to the patient: 'Well, you don't agree
with my interpretation. I still think it is right, although it may
be wrong. Perhaps we could see how it turns out' (p. 85). If
interpretation is a poetic process, one cannot simply assume
that one is right, for poetry relies on the viability of concepts,
the possibility of troping, not on clear and distinct meanings.
Indeed, such a process will include the making of mistakes,
since they provide negative clarification of what may be the
better choice of action.

Often using an apparently wayward style and technique,
Bion here demonstrates in general how to get access to the
particular unconscious of the patient. He declines to take any
statement at a univocal level: with a kind of benign deviance
he manages to foil any attempt on the part of the patient to

hold on to a single unequivocal interpretation. He deals with a variety of issues as they come up in each clinician's presentation. I shall now give three examples.

First, there is the problem of the patient who is initially fazed by the analyst's neutral front and never quite recovers from this feeling. Here, the patient continues to experience her session as a form of control, expressing anxiety about being made to 'stand still'. Bion outlines what he as analyst might say:

> We have here these chairs, this couch, because you might want to use any of them: you might want to sit in that chair, or you might want to lie on that couch in case you feel that you couldn't bear sitting there – as you say today. That is why this couch was here when you first came. I wonder what has made you discover this today. Why is it that only today you have found that you may not be able to sit in that chair; that you may have to lie down or go away? (pp. 4–5)

He adds that this intervention would come better in the first session, but also that 'every session is really a first session' and every day another day with no room for 'standing still'. Although the analyst will accept his patient as recognizably the same person each time they meet, the analytic couple are not a mother-and-baby couple, for the patient needs pressure to induce her not to remain frozen in an infantile posture. Thus in this particular case the analyst might consider:

> If I make allowances and say 'All right, sit in that chair if you want to', or 'Lie on the couch if you want to', will that patient make good use of that? Or will she feel that if I have allowed that much freedom, then she will take a bit more? For example, the patient can then say, 'Well, all right; if I can lie down here, I'm going to lie down and go to sleep. I'm going to have a never-ending analysis. I'm going to spend the rest of my life coming to you for analysis. I'll camp out in your house.' (p. 6)

Bion goes on to make this patient/analyst interaction a boundary issue. When the analyst tells him that the patient had an erotic dream of being face to face and mouth to mouth with her analyst, Bion comments, 'She can say, "I'd like that", but this depends on the belief that you wouldn't do anything [. . .] in other words, she wouldn't mind saying how much she would like sexual intercourse, or how much she would like to be alone with you, or her father, or her mother, provided she didn't have to do what fathers and mothers do' (p. 7). It is important, Bion concludes, that the patient learns to make 'a distinction between a fact when she is wide awake, and a fact when she is asleep', between dream and waking life, between a love affair and an analysis.

In inducing a facility of interpretation in the analyst Bion does not want to take over the analytic task himself, since he acknowledges that each analyst is in a privileged position which is not reproducible (cf. Spence in chapter 9 above), thus also keeping the boundaries between himself and his supervisees: 'There are millions of interpretations, but there is only one experience, and that is the experience which the analyst here had with this patient – while none of us had it' (p. 7). Bion wants to persuade the analyst, that (like the mother of Benjamin Spock fame) he must legitimate himself as the one who knows best what is good for his patient.

It is not as if Bion has to persuade both analyst and patient, because as supervisor he is not himself persuading the patient; he has rather to show the analyst that the proposed persuasion of the patient is an effective one. By demonstrating how the patient's unconscious meaning is present in what she says, he achieves this persuasion of the analyst. The rhetorical mode he employs in eliciting a change in interpretation of the analytic material becomes his mode of persuading the analyst. This command of a double rhetoric shows Bion to be not only a good analyst but also a good supervisor.

The second example focuses on the perennial question that the patient asks herself and her analyst: why does she come? In this case she says she comes to find out about herself. But, says Bion, she is not likely to ask a question to which she knows the answer. So, simply say 'You have posed the question' (p. 9) and wait until she has found the answer. The question can apply to both people in the room: when the patient asks why she comes she may wonder what the two people are there for and what they are doing. Perhaps there is a psychoanalytic explanation of why she wants to find out about herself. 'She has come into this room where there are two people and has started asking questions about what they are doing', as if there were 'a little girl watching what these people are up to'. If she asks a question and does not leave room for an answer 'because there is already an answer there', then there is no chance for either party to show curiosity about where the answer is. Here Bion delineates the dilemma of not having enough material for an interpretation, for then the patient can go in for a sort of blackmail, putting the analyst in the wrong: 'either he is so ignorant that he doesn't give any answers, or else so clever that he can do the job without any assistance' (p. 10):

> We are not trying to teach patients that we know all the answers, but that *if* they do the work they may find an answer. Nobody is going to do the work for them because no one can. (p. 11)

The analyst reports that the patient feels she is improving with him but then she says 'something unintelligible, as if she was eating the words' and speaks about the confusion in her mind (p. 11). Bion suggests the following might be said to her: 'You are feeling you take in my good analysis and turn it into a lot of confused stuff, and then you have to have more' (p. 12). He adds:

> If we were talking about the alimentary canal, we know that it takes a long time before a child connects what it eats with what it evacuates . . . Patients can feel as if they get good, clear analysis, but that it is turned into a lot of rubbish'.
>
> [. . .]
>
> What is one to say to the patient? [. . .] It is not simply a question of what you can understand, but whether this patient could understand an interpretation that you could give. To take a ridiculous example, you can't launch into a great explanation of the biology of the alimentary canal to a baby. It may be true, it may be the correct interpretation, but it is a nonsensical waste of time. (p. 12)

The rhetoric of this procedure consists in the way Bion conveys his advice to the analyst. It is a question of how the interpretation is made 'digestible' to the patient: the 'alimentary canal' is an image for the patient's psychic digestive system. The analyst has to find a modified form of his interpretation, pre-digested as food fit for a baby, or the baby/patient will shit out this good food/analysis. To forestall this waste, the analyst has to mediate his or her interpretation in such a way that it gets through the patient's defences. A transcription in the mind of the analyst of a particular patient's symptoms has to be retranscribed in order to reach the patient; the same interpretation of a similar problem in another patient would have to have a different retranscription to get through. An analyst has therefore to acquire specific translation skills to decipher the rhetoric of the psyche. On another level this is a practical illustration of Bion's basic psychoanalytic theory, wherein he postulates that the baby in its initial states is overwhelmed by 'beta elements', unconceptualized affective and sensory material, which the mother endeavours to transform by means of an 'alpha function' that orders brute experience into meaningful content, namely 'alpha elements' (thoughts).

Finally, in my third example, Bion draws on an analogy between psychoanalysis and aesthetic creation. The analyst's case material concerns a patient who has been rigid on the couch and, after a successful interpretation, feels 'untied', 'mentally more mobile'. Bion comments:

> One of the advantages of the patient's being able to feel better – it is very difficult to say what is meant by that, but it usually means some nice feeling – is that it gives a certain degree of confidence to go on having more analysis if there appears, in spite of these horrible feelings, a loosening of the fibres; it is a compensation. It is also one of these situations in which the presence of the analyst is very important – one always assumes that, but sometimes it becomes more apparent. In other words, while the patient is having a horrible fifty minutes, it is helpful to have the analyst present who is not feeling like that in the fifty minutes. (pp. 42–3)

With anxiety of disintegration comes a 'loosening of the fibres'. She is still fearful of what that loosening implies, perhaps something very primitive, like the state of being born.

> In the course of analysis – and in the course of life at large –
> people experience many 'rebirths' [. . .] In the analytic experi-
> ence you have the chance of seeing something which appears
> to be that kind of event – this upheaval in which the patient's
> attitude or personality seems to be changing. (p. 44)

On the one hand the fear helps her not to get rigid again, on
the other she is fearful of changes. The analyst can retain this
flexibility but the patient has difficulties:

> There is one way for the patient to deal with a situation like
> this: to make the movements of the outside – whatever it is –
> conform to the movements of the inside. And the same thing
> the other way round. If they conform absolutely, then there is
> no way of being aware of the uncomfortable conflict between
> the two. (p. 43)

But of course there is no such thing as an absolute conformity
between the two; sometimes the inside and sometimes the
outside has to give way. The analyst comments that if the patient could do it all by herself there would be no point in an
analysis (as indeed there would be no point in speaking if we
had everything we wanted). The analyst asks how he is to
convey this to the patient. Bion concedes the problem. He
uses a political analogy of how there will always be rebellion
within any existing system until the revolution itself becomes
part of the system. In the same way a great artist may appear
to rebel against the aesthetic canon but his revolution in turn
becomes part of it. The rebel does not rebel *in vacuo* but always has something to rebel against. There is always something resistant to be worked upon. This applies equally to the
analytic situation and the artistic one: there is material 'in which
we must learn to work' (p. 45). Bion compares the analytic
work with what the sculptor or artist has to do with his medium. Both analyst and sculptor must learn to respect their
medium. Neither can be a mere imitator, but has to be prepared to rebel against 'the accepted conventions':

> Once the representation by the human form, as done by
> Praxiteles in the Hermes, is accepted, someone like Rodin wants

to display not the classical, physical, external appearance of the human being, but something like the character or spirit. The situation repeats itself all the time: everybody sculpts just like Rodin. Of course, they may sculpt *just like* Rodin, but they are not Rodin. The same with painting: everybody agrees what a beautiful man or woman looks like. Then there comes along a Picasso who draws people he says are men and women, but who seem to have no conformity with the anatomical structure with which we are all familiar. Then it becomes the accepted style to paint 'just like' Picasso. (p. 45)

Something original and creative must be done with the material, while at the same time its limitations must still be respected, for it is only within these limitations that the artist/analyst can be creative.[2] It is no use imagining that a template can be used to check what happens. Imitators who try to sculpt like Rodin will fail: only those who find the style to communicate their visions will be able to liberate 'this mass of material' that is the medium for both the analytic and the artistic process.

In Lacanian terms, the real of the patient has to be respected if it is to be brought within symbolic bounds. Indeed, Lacan defines respect as not getting too close to that in the subject which denies castration, to that which is most particular in every subject. Thus the rhetoric of the clinical session is here spelt out as a rhetoric of the poetic process, and the clinical encounter as an opportunity for what is a form of aesthetic creation.

Salvador Minuchin

Salvador Minuchin works in the USA as a 'structural family therapist',[3] engaging with the family constellation and its interrelational dynamics rather than with the individual as a separate monad. He looks at the family's ongoing 'transactional patterns (p. 91), in which he detects positions of dominance and submission that betray dysfunctional behaviours. In particular he has worked with families where there is a case of anorexia nervosa and where the 'identified patient' presents in a concealed fashion the family's predicament (p. 112). The emphasis is on the way in which family members communicate with each other, but, unlike other family therapists who emphasize the role play within the family, Minuchin explores the power relations embedded in the communication structure of the family in question. His strategy is not to comment from outside but to enter into the existing dialogue in an attempt to break up the collusions that maintain the current dysfunction. By this means he endeavours both to identify and to reconstruct the communicative matrix wherein the power is lodged. His participation in the family dialogue is the rhetorical instrument whereby he reconstitutes the matrix and thus allows the family members to speak from new positions. When Minuchin approaches his families, he does not directly tell the family what is wrong with them but involves himself in the dynamics by means of indirect suggestion, as if he were a stage director with a cast with whom he is rehearsing. To get the best out of actors a director does not specify what is to be done but looks out for commitments and betrayals that can be developed, sometimes as a comedian would do, by suggesting another context for what has been said, and sometimes by carrying to excess the implications of someone's remarks.

As an example I shall discuss one of his family cases in an attempt to identify the characteristic style of Minuchin's rhetoric.[4] The Menotti family, an Italian-American family, consists of father (Carlo, an unskilled civil servant), mother (Margherita, a housewife), their anorexic daughter (Loretta, aged sixteen), and four other children, two of whom are present at the consultation interview. Loretta has been repeatedly hospitalized from the age of thirteen, her weight finally dropping to 75 pounds. At the time of the interview she is depressed and has not been to school for several months.

In the initial exchange it is already clear that the parents speak for their daughter. When she is asked how long she has been losing weight, the father corrects his daughter's statement, and the mother presents herself as an effective caretaker of her daughter, the one who takes on the world for her:

So I take Loretta home, because I don't want nobody to touch my daughter. So I take her home, and next day Loretta throws up. She cries. She has a pain. So I call the car service, put Loretta in the car, and take her to Dr Smith. (p. 283)

Minuchin continues with the interview, trying to give Loretta the beginnings of some degree of autonomy: 'I would like to know from your point of view, Loretta. What was it that you were having?' (p. 283). But then he takes the opportunity to reinstate and also inventively redefine the function of the mother: 'Since Mother is the memory of the family, she will tell you, but you will need to check it, because it's your life she is describing' (p. 283). Minuchin indicates to Loretta the need to correct a concept from one's own point of view. The discussion then circles around what happened while Loretta stayed in hospital:

MOTHER: So I stay two weeks with Loretta in the hospital.

MINUCHIN: You stayed in the hospital with her?

FATHER: Yes, she spent many nights with her.

MINUCHIN: But, Mr Menotti, didn't you miss her?

FATHER: Well, I did miss her, but we managed to go on, you know –

MINUCHIN: What about the little ones? Who handled Giuseppi and Enrico?

SOPHIA and MARIA (in unison): Both of us. (p. 284)

After eliciting how much the mother's bossiness affects the other members of the family, the therapist comments: 'That's wonderful. Okay, and Mother stayed two weeks in the hospital. My goodness, that's an Italian heart for you' (p. 285). The mother takes this rhetorical concession to the value she has in the family as a cue to tell the story of how she had divined that something was not right with her daughter and had issued a challenge to the hospital (which now transferentially includes the therapist): 'What do you mean, nothing is wrong with Loretta? She's all black and blue' (p. 285).

Minuchin sees the mother's discourse as a graphic description of a mother/daughter fusion unusual outside psychotic phenomena and in the interspersed dialogue with an inter-

viewer puts it down 'to the position of the mother in the peas-
ant culture of southern Italy', here conflicting with the contemporary culture and thus trapping the daughter into a double
bind.

Minuchin waits for the opportunity to capitalize on the reassurance he gave the mother (saying 'she can hear vibrations
from the hospital') in order to challenge her by troping on her
'big heart' ('do you think that Mama has too big a heart and
that sometimes that makes her worry more than is necessary?')
and following up with a shift from one organ to another ('I
think Margherita is deaf in this ear'). This rhetoric enables
him to make an attempt to shift the power relations within
this family. But it is uphill work:

> FATHER: Well, what I've seen, Mama does herself much of the
> things the girls could do by themselves. She makes it too easy
> for them. Now they find it a little hard to begin to manage by
> themselves and try out this situation.
>
> MINUCHIN: That's a very interesting and very sensitive view. Can
> you say it again, because I think Margherita is deaf in this ear?
>
> FATHER: I am sure Margherita understood already what I'm talk-
> ing about.
>
> MINUCHIN: Do you understand what he says? What do you think
> about that?
>
> MOTHER: Why do I have to think? I am a mother. The things
> they can't do, I do.
>
> MINUCHIN: If the kids say do something, you do.
>
> MOTHER: What am I to do? – let the kids down?
>
> MINUCHIN: Now, what about what Carlo says, that you do more
> than what they need?
>
> FATHER: You've been doing, and you don't mind doing anything
> for them, right?
>
> MOTHER: I don't. I help my kids all the time in all ways. If they
> want help, my kids, I give it to them. That's what I do for my
> kids, then, all the time. (p. 289)

The therapist tries to enlist the father as an ally ('I think you
still did not hear clearly what your husband has said and what

Loretta has said'). This encourages the daughter to challenge the mother's resistance to change:

> LORETTA: To things that you already know about, everything is yes. But to things that are new to you, it's always no. You don't want to hear about it. (p. 290)

The daughter is now able to develop this rhetorical challenge to the mother's supremacy in the family, and in particular the battle is about whose language is to prevail:

> LORETTA: We use certain words and you don't understand them. You know your own meanings for them and you misunderstand what one of us is trying to say to you, and when we explain to you what the real thing is, you don't want to hear about it and won't unless it was the way you said it. (p. 295)

Loretta is here registering her complaint that her otherness, the 'real thing', as invested in the meanings she gives to words, is not recognized by her mother who is still bound by the 'old country' milieu and its culture as against the 'new country' that the daughter is inhabiting. It is important to see that Minuchin supports the daughter's rebellion on the level of speech rather than that of eating. The collusively distorted duo of mother and daughter is invaded by the therapist who thereby disturbs the 'triangulation' of two against one (p. 33), which has hitherto excluded the father. Minuchin is thereby inserting himself into a space which he hopes will in future be occupied by the father, his aim being to activate family sub-systems at different levels, that is, to develop groupings that protect and further the subsidiary rights of family members, giving them scope to form new alliances, a 'de-triangulation'. The character of the existing collusion is to be seen in the daughter's presenting herself symptomatically as a victim of anorexia in an unconscious acceptance of (and conscious rebellion against) the directiveness of the mother, which keeps the father at arm's length from them both. To counter this ploy the therapist repeatedly tries to bring the mother and the father into open conflict:

> FATHER: But this is not the point.
> MOTHER: That's the point, Loretta went out.
> FATHER: The point is that you undermine me. (p. 298)

The father here shows his rhetorical competence by changing the context around the very word 'point', which indicates the focus of a rhetorical exchange. Nevertheless, he is still enmeshed in the avoidance of conflict, continuing to retreat from anger into self-pity. What the couple are unable to do is to turn conflict into negotiation, in that they flinch away from the acknowledgement of their own anger, which Loretta is soaking up. This is the context of the symptom of her refusal to eat – the stage on which she habitually conducts her rebellion. Minuchin's efforts are directed towards showing the daughter that her rebellion needs to be conducted on another level than that of the symptom (i.e., that of the 'identified patient'), since the rebellion has lost its effectiveness through the mother's increasing awareness of the anorexia as part of the power struggle, rather than as a focus of worry and concern:

> MOTHER: She wins me all the time, my daughter. Do you know by what? Because I say something, 'Loretta, we have to do this.' 'Oh no, Mama, we have to do this.' I say. 'No.' Loretta then she stop eating, because we have to do it Loretta's way all the time. (p. 307)

Loretta's 'sickness' is here redefined as 'badness', which Loretta objects to since it redesignates her place in the family from an object of care to one of disapproval, 'the black sheep of the family' (p. 309). Minuchin does not condone the childishness of her behaviour but also indicts the family for being complicit in it. To show them how to get out of the trap he joins in the family lunch, which enables him to arrange that the daughter eat alone in the immediate future and endeavour to keep her weight at a constant level, while instructing the family that no reference is to be made to her food habits. At the same time he instructs Loretta to set aside regular time to talk to her father with the object of achieving a measure of separation from the mother.

His method is not to offer the family an interpretation of their behaviour, since this would not foster the necessary unconscious interaction which only the family itself can bring about, but to engage in ongoing improvised interventions which include him in the process of restructuring the power relations within the family. The troping skills of Minuchin, like those of a theatrical producer, consist of comments which redirect the interpretation in which the identifications of the participants are involved. Each utterance of the family constitutes a claim upon identity, and Minuchin's interventions obliquely indicate its hypothetical nature, largely by skilfully feeding back his creative response to that hypothesis, which he often imputes to other family members for whom he thus unobviously speaks. He thereby manages to begin a reconstruction of the identities within the group, noticing when a member of the family is too dominant or too submissive. This produces constant troping of the speech of the participants without engaging in direct contradiction and achieves a rhetorical persuasion which is in fact his clinical management of the situation.

12

Out of tune: Elfriede Jelinek's The Piano Teacher

With the advent of modern critical theory the author as 'sub-ject-supposed-to-know' (Lacan's term for the knowledge the patient imputes to the analyst) has had to share her or his authority with the reader/critic. All are 'writing' from a posi-tion in desire, that is, governed by what the Other desires. Since one can never wholly anticipate how another will read, from the viewpoint of the symbolic this process inevitably produces failures of meaning, gaps in the text. Hence, modern reader theory and practice has been preoccupied in various ways with theorizing gaps in the literary and historical text: the question is how they are to be filled.[1] This does not neces-sarily mean that writer or reader is any less disposed to give up the position of master/mistress of the gaps, but that the text as a site of transferential meanings has learnt to look after itself, that is to say, as it is being read it still preserves some autonomy. Indeed, the literary text runs a smaller risk at the hands of the psychoanalyst than the patient does. Neither the treatment of Edgar Allan Poe by Marie Bonaparte[2] nor that of the Mona Lisa by Freud[3] has disfigured these texts for all time, but, on the contrary, has given rise to what has been called the 'Poe-etic effect'.[4]

What happens when a writer takes a clinical case as her subject, thus producing a virtual clinical case? There will be troping, rereading and reassignment of meaning on two levels, that of the case itself and that of the fictional presentation of the case: the literary character as a patient will be betraying the poetics of her unconscious through the fictional life she has been given and she will also be created through the author's and reader's entering into the poetics of the text, the language that is always in excess. The literary character Erica's cutting herself – her symptom – is the trope of the patient: the figuration that Elfriede Jelinek employs, 'the arduously tamed blood rushes out from behind the barrier' (p. 44), is the means by which the fictional effect is created, now both trope and symptom of the text.[5]

The book begins on this dual note of pathology and fiction:

> Erica, the meadow flower. That's how she got her name: *erica*. Her pregnant mother had visions of something timid and tender. Then, seeing the lump of clay that shot out of her body, she promptly began to mould it relentlessly to keep it pure and fine. Remove a bit here, a bit there. Every child instinctively heads towards filth and dirt unless you pull it back. (pp. 23–4)

The text hereby proclaims the dialectic that produces this pathology: a rigid cultural ideal versus the stubborn materiality of life. The clay resists the ideal despite the insistence of the letter, the naming of Erica as meadow flower. This dialectic exceeds the speech and thoughts of the text's individual figures; they are spoken for and about by a heterogeneous narrative voice that continually changes point of view, luring the reader by its blatant display of recognizable scenarios and pathologies. It is a text which at first sight opens itself to a number of psychoanalytic readings[6] but subsequently proves curiously resistant. The text even flaunts its own meta-commentary:

> Erica is in the pink of health – a well-nourished fish in her mother's amniotic fluid. (p. 56)

> She knows that her mother's embrace will completely devour and digest her yet she is magically drawn to it. (p. 118)

Erica Kohut is a piano teacher, a fact unambiguously stated in the English translation of the title. The German title, *Die Klavierspielerin*, insinuates that she might have achieved the status of a concert pianist designed for her by her mother, instead of remaining in the lower ranks as a piano teacher at the Vienna Conservatoire. Erica is in her late thirties and lives with her mother, sharing the parental bed; soon after Erica's birth the father became feeble-minded and was transferred to an institution. Mother and daughter are fused in a symbiotic union, undisturbed by any third party, with Mother (spelt with an initial capital throughout) vetoing every male approach. The mother, undeterred by Erica's failure to live up to her hopes, continues to tempt the daughter with narcissistic iden-tifications (the name 'Kohut' inscribes a connection with the American psychologist of the self, an analyst of narcissistic disorders).[7] She constantly reinforces her claim to the daugh-ter, yet at the same time endeavours to instil in her a sense of uniqueness and superiority, encoded in the text by the inter-mittent capitalization of the third person singular pronoun:

> The hawk mother and the buzzard grandmother order the child, their charge, not to leave the eyrie. They cut off HER life in thick slices. (p. 34)

> SHE is the exception to the norm that surrounds her repul-sively. (p. 15)

The symbiotic union of mother and daughter is thus classi-cally undermined by a double-bind which extends into a gen-eral textual strategy. For while the text insistently proffers the pathology of individual characters, its case-history aspect, its narrative undecidability (who speaks in the opening para-graph?) and its intertextuality (the traces of other texts within it) repeatedly undermine the search for character- or author-viewpoints whereby a reader might position herself. Hence, the reader too is caught in a double-bind, hystericized by the textual strategies, unable to find a firm vantage point. The German reader, in particular, will be implicated in how the text irreverently incorporates the most canonized of national idealist thinkers, poets and composers, only to spit them out again, together with their notions of the bourgeois liberated subject. For instance, Goethe's idea that salvation is ruled out if the Faustian subject attains the Faustian object of desire and stops striving for the ultimate experience[8] is relentlessly parodied, appropriated at a(n) (im)pertinent moment, just when the young Erica is caught up in lecherous play with a favoured male cousin, who has her kneeling before him:

> the red genital pouch sways and dangles, it swings seductively before Her eyes [. . .] SHE is the addressee of this package, [. . .] SHE peers and peers [. . .] Just let this moment linger, it's so good. (pp. 42–3)

The final sentence denotes the ultimate (and forbidden) moment of satisfaction (Faust's 'Remain, so fair art thou, remain!').

Canonized cultural institutions are similarly desecrated, exposed to the play of the signifier, in particular, music, the most idealized symbolic discourse, and Germany/Austria, as its holiest of shrines:

> Erica jeers at the student's Bach. It is a muddy creek [*Bächlein*], faltering over obstacles like small rocks and mounds, stumbling along in its dirty bed. [. . .] Deliberately trying to humiliate the student, Erica praises Bach's work to the skies. She claims that Bach rebuilds gothic cathedrals wherever his music is played. Erica feels a tingling between her legs, something felt only by those chosen by and for art when they talk about art. (pp. 100–1)

The text gleefully reveals the silent workings of the material in what is presumed to be ideal. Instead of luring the subject with a vision of union of mind and body, spirit and matter, freedom and determinism, the text deconstructs the old metaphysics of nature, love and sexuality. It turns on its head the ideology of the traditional aesthetic, discerning in it a stale imaginary, a fantasy of primary narcissism, and reveals that, to take Terry Eagleton's words, 'there is something in the body which can revolt against the power which inscribes it'.[9] *The Piano Teacher* shows graphically that the body is not at home in language, that bodies, far from being autonomous, are bound up with other bodies: 'She is flesh of this flesh! A crumb of the maternal cake. [. . .] She winds around Mother like ivy around an old house, but this Mother is definitely not a cosy old house' (p. 233). For Eagleton, 'the aesthetic concerns this most gross and palpable dimension of the human, which post-Cartesian philosophy, in some curious lapse of attention, has somehow managed to overlook [. . .] the body's long inarticulate rebellion against the tyranny of the theoretical.'[10]

A psychoanalytic reading appropriate for this text might therefore draw on those theories which insist that at the level of lived experience there is something unrepresentable which stubbornly remains and which does not appear solely in pathological symptoms. There is Lacan's insistence, after Alexandre Kojève, that 'the symbol manifests itself first of all in the murder of the thing',[11] by which he indicates that the very abstraction of the concept must retreat from sensible reality, defeated by the unrepresentable. However, this unrepresentable is not some mystical essence which could refer back to the very idealism the text throws out and throws up in disgust, but a leftover of the real, an excess of *jouissance*, an overflow of libido that seeks an endless intensity, perversely over-indulging the pleasure-body in compensation for the traumatic failure of discourse to match the physical body. And just as physical bodies exhibit symptoms of civilization's discontents, so do textual bodies. The unconscious of the text might then be sought at the level of the textual body – the word – rather than at the level of its individual characters. Just as with the readings of the case histories already discussed, a reading of the textual body can show that the unconscious is irrepressible even in a text which plots the capture of the subject in the symbolic – the 'music teacher'.

In *The Piano Teacher* there is an implicit invitation to the reader to participate in a perverse pleasure. An excess of libido shows itself in alarming and disgusting overflows of every kind of bodily fluid, with a constant erosion of boundaries:

> For an instant, a slit gapes in the previously intact tissue; then the arduously tamed blood rushes out from behind the barrier. [. . .] Bright red blood trickles and trails from the wounds,

sullying everything as it flows. It oozes, warm, silent, and the sensation is not unpleasant. It's so liquid. It runs incessantly. [. . .] On and on. It runs and runs and runs. (p. 44)

The aperture gapes, terrified at the change, and blood pours out. [. . .] The drops ooze, run, blend with their comrades, turning into a red trickle, then a soothingly steady red stream when the individual trickles unite. The blood prevents HER from seeing what she has sliced open. It was her own body, but it was dreadfully alien to her. (pp. 86–7)

The body has gone into reverse gear, refusing borders and limits; there is an enjoyment of those modes of corporeality which Julia Kristeva calls 'the improper/unclean':[12]

She neatly trims the frazzled edges of nearby objects that explode, detonate, or simply lie still, and she takes them over, combing their seams, looking for crumbs, dirt, or torn-off bits to analyse, if possible before their lives are taken to the cleaners. There's so much to seek and find. For Erica, these chips and snips are the true gist. (p. 127)

Objects here represent *a fortiori* the definitions imposed by the symbolic. The explosion and detonation of these objects figure both a fearful and a terroristic rejection; seams are boundaries where something has been sewn together, but these bear evidence of failure, signifying what Kristeva calls 'fluid demarcations of yet unstable territories'.[13] They are being inspected for the repulsive waste material that lodges there, disturbing 'identity, system, order',[14] which are presumed to be in the service of life and the failure of which is associated with death. Jelinek writes in an effort to explain the real of the body, its excessive presence:

Erica hates that porous, rancid fruit that marks the bottom of her abdomen. [. . .] Soon the decay will progress, encroaching upon the larger parts of her body. Then she will die in torment. Dismayed, Erica pictures herself as a numb hole, six feet of space, disintegrating in the earth. The hole that she despised and neglected has now taken full possession of her. She is nothing. And there is nothing left for her. (p. 198)

For Kristeva, the corpse is 'the utmost of abjection',[15] here linked with a refusal of sexual difference. The figure in the text that conjoins death, gender and sexuality is a hole. The text seems to ask for a reduction of the body: there is abjection of the reproductive function itself as a 'rancid fruit', and hence, elsewhere, not surprisingly, a rejection of romantic love as a sublimation of that function. One of Erica's students has been pursuing her, with increasingly unpredictable behaviour on both sides:

> Walter Klemmer is truly in love. [. . .] His love, however, is unrequited. [. . .] This turns his stomach, and he proves his disgust by hawking up mucus and noisily placing it in the sink. Klemmer's love placenta [. . .] Since Klemmer doesn't rinse the sink, his clams linger at the drain hole. (p. 122)

Slime, spit, semen, mucus, urine and so on are all boundary phenomena, in two senses: they are amorphous, and they are produced at the rims of the body, through a hole. There is both horror of the undifferentiated and a revelling in disgust. *Jouissance*, the field of libido, challenges the phallic proscription and rends apart the textual body in a defiant gesture: the body sends a symptomatic message to the symbolic that it rejects sexual difference and in particular the codification of feminine desire as a figure of lack.

In a display of psychotic symptoms the text presents a pleasure in amorphous bodily substances, an excessive figuration of dissolution, of dis-figuration. Poetic language is thereby deprived of its traditional/familiar aesthetic and instead assumes the form of a psychotic-aesthetic language where pleasure is taken in disgust: since the symbolic has so little to offer, the text refuses to invest it with libido except via disgust. As noted already, a prime target in the symbolic is German idealist thinking. The sacrilege of disgust is performed upon every aspect of it, in particular its constitution of a 'second nature', on a higher level, where matter and form, inclination and duty, would be at one. This inaugurates a series of subversive turns, whereby the old binaries of natural/unnatural, real/unreal, art/commodity are shown to be ideological constructs. Consider, for example, the occasion when mother and daughter take a nature walk on the outskirts of Vienna:

> This is like the days of Eichendorff, Mother chirps, the important thing is your spirit, your attitude to nature. Nature itself is secondary! The two women have the proper spirit for they are able to delight in nature whenever they catch sight of it. If they stumble upon a rippling brook, they instantly drink water from it. Let's hope no deer has pissed into it. If they come to a thick tree or dense underbrush, they can take a piss themselves, and the non-pisser stands guard to ward off any impudent peepers. (p. 32)

Nature is not 'pure' in the way ideology perceives it, since its organic processes make it unfit for human consumption, while the human subject is 'free' to pollute it as long as it observes the proprieties fitting for its higher nature (no 'impudent peepers'). Culture thus redefines nature, installing a symbolic which turns out to be imaginary: nature is in fact nothing but a pathetic fallacy, indifferent to the fervent endeavours of the human subject to find itself confirmed in it. Thus the bungled sexual efforts of Erica and her would-be student-lover:

> A low treetop beyond the window. A chestnut tree. The tastelessness of Klemmer's sourballs inside her oral cavity, as the man, moaning senselessly, presses his all into her face. Erica sees an almost imperceptible swaying of the branches down below as they start to get besieged by raindrops. [. . .] Next, an inaudible patter, then a downpour. [. . .] The man is still stuffing himself into the woman's mouth, clutching her hair and her ears, while on the outside, natural forces rule with an overwhelming power. She still wants and he still can't. (p. 245)

However, the text's most compelling move does not, as one has come to expect, reside strictly in its masterful ideological turning of the tables, but in those abundant places where it compulsively turns disgust into perverse pleasure. Culture has failed in its endeavour to impress itself on nature. The sadomasochistic rituals prescribed by Erica in the letter she sends to Klemmer perform exactly this failure of the symbolic. The

letter enacts a fantasized severity of the symbolic, the orders
in it miming the dreaded Other in a vain attempt to present it
as complicit with desire:

> Her most haunting wish – the adored Herr Klemmer reads – is
> for you to punish me. She would like Klemmer as a punish-
> ment. And in such a way that he ties her up with the ropes I've
> collected, also the leather straps and even the chains! Hogtie
> her, bind her up as thoroughly as he can – solidly, intensely,
> artfully, cruelly, tormentingly, cunningly. He could bore his
> knees into her abdomen, if you'll be so kind. (p. 215)

The fluctuation in the pronouns in this passage, indicating that
the enunciation changes from third person to first, signals
Erica's ambivalence towards her fantasy. She wants to be in
two incompatible positions, determined ('punished' by him)
and determining (giving orders to 'you'), the classic masochist
manœuvre. The Kantian imperative – as the Idealists read him,
to achieve by a voluntary act a perfect match of duty and
inclination, is here stood on its head: the harshest repression
('bore his knees into her abdomen') must guarantee the most
intense bliss ('if you'll be so kind'), turning the imperative,
the command, into a sadomasochistic contract. But this would
make Kant into the truth of Sade. According to Lacan, however, although both Kant and Sade see the subject as an autonomous legislator of its own morality, Kant insisted that each
subject should be treated with respect (*Achtung*) as an end-
in-itself, whereas Sade's subject assigns its own internal division to the victim it punishes. Lacan is here showing up the
paradox of the symbolic, that it hides its driving force, the
unconscious pursuit of an (obscene) enjoyment in inducing
suffering in the other.[16] Erica's acceptance of repression is the
warrant for her bliss, her desire to submit to symbolic authority. This dilemma leads to the climax of the 'plot', where the
fantasy is shattered through turning into actual violence in a
scene of rape, bodily harm and total abandonment.

It is here that the text disturbingly transmogrifies into an
allegory of the suffering single bourgeois subject, as if the perverse pleasure the reader is invited to share depended on the
satire of old Vienna and its outworn shibboleths, whereas the

book performs a violent attack on the symbolic order *per se*. Even though the text within itself shows a blatant self-reflexive awareness of the dynamics of psychosis at the level of character, at the level of its allegory it shows an indulgence to the very excess it castigates. It presents a world, an ahistorical wasteland despite all its 'history', constructed around the daughter, excluding the subjectivities of mothers, fathers, sons and lovers. Instead of confronting the problematic of the body's real and imaginary relations to the symbolic, the text perversely uses the narrative of its own symptomology to allegorize the destruction of the bourgeois subject, expending its energies in attacking a favoured political target. The old symbolic boundaries excite a violent disgust which turns into *jouissance* as blockage of libido is released, but, instead of this being used to create new signifiers, it perversely turns back on itself for a renewed onslaught in an orgy of destruction of the symbolic. Neither the symbolic nor the imaginary offers any ideals, goals or visions to internalize: the Law is discredited and rejected, and there are no new subjective models wherewith to construct an alternative. The aesthetics of disgust remains trapped in a rejection of a signifier for the Law. Thus, ultimately, the 'lump of clay', the text, although it has taken the radical mould, bears the mark of reactionary deformation.

The figurality of the text thus lends itself to clinical and textual readings on two levels, that of Erica (as case and literary character) and that of the text as a whole (as case and literary achievement).

On the level of a clinical case, had Erica presented herself for psychoanalysis, she would most likely have been classified as being a 'borderline' by a Freudian analyst and as having a psychotic structure by a Lacanian. As a borderline, Erica Kohut would have to have had a childhood 'marked by a lack of gratifying responses and by the scarcity of usable ideals. [. . .] Heinz Kohut in particular insists on the fact that a positive sense of self depends on the loving gaze of the other, usually the maternal selfobject'.[17] Within a Lacanian orientation Erica's cutting herself could indicate an attempt at castration due to a foreclosure of the Name-of-the-Father, Lacan's signifier for the Law, and the treatment would be in the direction of finding a supplement, a framework, a kind of Lacanian 'holding', which would help her to construct an imaginary world without the help of the Name-of-the-Father, giving her the semblance of a 'real' place. On the level of the literary character, Erica's symptoms are represented as cultural discontent: she is the victim, albeit ironically portrayed, of an establishment, both parental ('she knows that her mother's embrace will completely devour and digest her') and cultural ('the important thing is your spirit, your attitude to nature').

On the textual level (which exceeds that of any single character) the clinical diagnosis is similarly that of a psychotic formation since there has also been a rejection of a signifier for the Law. Here the symptoms emerge in the pleasure that is taken in disgust; it is pleasurable to set up Vienna and bourgeois humanism as satirical targets. The fictional effect, different from that of a case history, is the ironic mask that is relentlessly maintained, the unforgivingness towards the social. However, the transcendence of the fictional over the clinical is a creative transformation which is not necessarily edifying, since the psychotic effect is allowed to prevail.[18] The poetic effect of the fictional resides rather in the effect of a negation, in that there is a disgust at the disgust – at its very excess. This effect can be attributed to the extraordinary creative potential of this text, though the pathology it figures both in and through its characters and through its overall figuration reveals its own unconscious end to attack the symbolic.

Conclusion

The notion of 'the text' as a site of transferential meanings developed, as discussed above, in the wake of Saussure's theory of language, but despite the revolutionary effect of his work, which did away with any simple referential theory of meaning, it took some time to account for the problem of the real that lies under all the objects referred to in the text. From the viewpoint of the real, which psychoanalysis theorizes as that part of the subject that has escaped the signifier of language, there remains a problematic excess that overflows the symbolic, namely, the unconscious, and it is at these margins of language that the unconscious makes itself felt. Neither writer nor reader, analysand nor analyst, will know in advance what referential effects will be brought into play in the course of a reading or session. What happens is that the unconscious does its own reading: it 'reads' by means of verbal associations and sounds that attach themselves to networks of images which come from early bodily experience.

These unconscious effects have been theorized in different ways, in Freud's terms as primary process, in Lacan's as the real, in Kristeva's as the semiotic, but whatever the theoretical differences might be, the unconscious invades the supposedly objective and rational language system. This excess of signification – experienced also as a gap in meaning, because it is always out of place – is omitted from Saussure's theory of language, Jakobson's communication model, and Speech Act theory. For both psychoanalysis and literary theory, the focus

is on textuality, the condensations and displacements (metaphors and metonymies) of language in the production of desire. This invariably produces conflict, since the literary/analytic
text is desired on the one hand as Law, the language of the
symbolic, giving the subject its sexual identification, and on
the other as a site of continual search for the lost object. Thus
meaning is never final, and textual analysis is as unpredictable
as life analysis.

The continual search and the inevitable failure to find en-
genders the never-ending process of mourning, a recurring
theme. Words themselves are a form of mourning, because
they fail to deliver the promise they appear to make. Each
word contains a commitment of desire which will to some
degree be denied: hence, whenever we speak, we mourn the
partial non-fulfilment of desire. Since words thus fail to capture the world, they also fail to capture the perfect reader
(since there will never be one), time overtaking all meaning.
All language is at the mercy of memory, the body's attempt to
monumentalize its experiences into safe repetitions, which
inevitably fail. *Hamlet* is an excellent source of illustration for
the name as already 'wounded', as already its own epitaph,
with Hamlet unable to take his father's name.[1] Words or names
as promises are already broken, because they are always excessive, grasping more than they are meant to bear.

Given the treachery of language, troubling alike analysts,
analysands, readers and writers, it is unfortunate that there
are still impediments to a fertile dialogue between psychoanalysts and literary-critical theorists.[2] Both the clinical and
literary discourses displace and condense the usual binary
oppositions like female/male, passive/active, slave/master. In
Edward Lear's 'The Owl and the Pussy-Cat', who takes the
dominant role in the owl's courtship of the pussy-cat? In the
analytic/reading situation, who 'seduces' whom? The seductive effect of the text on the reader has been classically dem-
onstrated in Roland Barthes' *The Pleasure of the Text*,[3] and the
seductive effect of the analyst on the analysand and vice versa
has been amply documented in the analytic literature on transference and countertransference. Can psychoanalytic and literary 'free association' – that psychic/poetic inspiration of the

analytic process – be securely lodged on one side or the other? Can literary theory adequately account for the multiple meanings generated by the text without a theory of the unconscious? Can psychoanalysis adequately account for the uncanny shifts of meaning that occur from moment to moment in a clinical session without a modern theory of language?

The parallels abound. But, as a last-ditch objection – the usual attack when it is a matter of applied versus clinical psychoanalysis – how can you put a text on the couch when it cannot answer back? The question finally arises: to what extent does the reader's relationship to the text have any equivalence with the relationship between analyst and analysand? One of the standard objections is that the text does not have an unconscious, only persons do; and, even if the author has, you cannot put him or her on the couch. Psychoanalysts themselves have been sceptical about the contributions of literary and critical theory to their discourse. The assumption is that somehow the analysand is in a position to verify the analyst's interpretation in a straightforward way, instead of there being a dialectical interchange, where the utterance of both parties is material for further interpretation, destabilized by its reference to the Other, to language and Law to which both parties are subject. What is forgotten in this assumption is that the analytic text – the psychoanalytic dialogue – is an uncanny object, as hard to pin down as the analytic cure. Both literary and analytic texts (those of authors and critics, of analysts and analysands) have to prove themselves again and again in the world: all parties will continue to treat their respective texts and each other's texts with suspicion. At the same time, their ministrations keep their own texts and those of their uncanny doubles alive. Although one should not assume that therapy cannot be done on art and literature,[4] in the sense that criticism can bring a work back to life, I do not see the critic's task as necessarily affirming a poem's unity, though there is always a temptation to do that (perhaps illustrated in my effort to find sense in Edward Lear's nonsense). A creative reading of texts and patients might also be a moment of dismantling, of taking apart (analysing) without being in a hurry to put together, to achieve what deconstruction has termed 'closure'.

In the often negative transferential relations between psycho-analysis and literary theory, it is a pity that neither seems to be able to renounce their fantasy of the other as inhabiting a realm from which they are by definition excluded and which they must therefore either conquer or discredit. Both dis-courses would do well to take note of those current develop-ments in other fields – in rhetoric, psycholinguistics, politics, social theory and philosophy – where the intersubjective con-struction of subjects and objects has become the focus of at-tention.

Both art/literature and psychoanalysis create things with-out knowing what they will be, using a concrete material which will work both for and against the creative subject. If the re-sult of their creative effort were known in advance, there would be no point in engaging in it. Experience is always blind and knowledge comes after the event, retrospectively, *nachträglich*, as a painful troping of an earlier identity. The paradox of the unconscious is that it yields a knowledge which does not al-low for knowing that one knows; it knows itself only in errors and slips. The poetics of the unconscious make use of a 'rhe-torical overload':[5] the 'literary' is that language which makes something heard other than what it says; by the same token, psychoanalysis is a literary practice of language. In either case, the text organizes our disappointment.[6] All the subject can name is a rhetorical substitute. As Freud has amply demon-strated in his interpretation of dreams and symptoms, trans-ference is the only way an unconscious idea can get into consciousness – by transferring its intensity to an idea that is already there. It is the analyst's/poet's task to reconcile the analysand/reader to her or his own particular rhetoric.

Notes

(PFL stands for the Pelican Freud Library)

Introduction

1   Maud Ellmann, *Psychoanalytic Literary Criticism* (London and New York, Longman, 1994), p. 26.

2   Jacques Derrida, *The Postcard: From Socrates to Freud and Beyond*, trans. Alan Bass (Chicago and London, Chicago University Press, 1987 [French original 1980]).

3   Shoshana Felman, 'To open the question', in *Literature and Psychoanalysis. The Question of Reading: Otherwise, Yale French Studies*, 55–6 (1977), pp. 5–10.

4   John Crowe Ransom, *The New Criticism* (Norfolk, Virginia, New Directions, 1941 [first published 1938]); Cleanth Brooks, *The Well-Wrought Urn: Studies in the Structure of Poetry* (London, Methuen, 1968 [first published 1947]).

5   Wayne C. Booth, *The Rhetoric of Fiction* (Chicago and London, Chicago University Press, 1961).

6   Noam Chomsky, *Aspects of the Theory of Syntax*, Cambridge, Massachusetts, MIT Press, 1965, p. 21: 'If a sentence such as "flying planes can be dangerous" is presented in an appropriately constructed context, the listener will interpret it immediately in a unique way, and will fail to detect the ambiguity. In fact, he may reject the second interpretation, when this is pointed out to him, as forced or unnatural (independently of which interpretation he originally selected under contextual pressure). Nevertheless, his intuitive knowledge of the language is clearly such that both of the interpretations (corresponding

to "flying planes is dangerous" and "flying planes are dangerous") are assigned to the sentence by the grammar he has inter-
nalized in some form.' For a fuller grammatical explanation see
Chomsky, *The Logical Structure of Linguistic Theory*, New York
and London, Plenum Press, 1975), p. 178.

Chapter 1   What is a psychoanalytic reading?

Some of the material in this chapter has appeared in a different
form in *The Edinburgh Encyclopedia of Continental Philosophy*, ed.
Simon Glendinning (Edinburgh, Edinburgh University Press, 1990).

1 Jean Laplanche and Jean-Bertrand Pontalis, *The Language of
   Psychoanalysis*, trans. Daniel Lagache (London, The Hogarth
   Press and the Institute of Psycho-Analysis, 1973 [French origi-
   nal 1967]), pp. 331–3.
2 Sigmund Freud, 'Three essays on sexuality', in *On Sexuality:
   Three Essays on the Theory of Sexuality and Other Works*, ed.
   Angela Richards (Harmondsworth, Penguin Books, 1977), vol.
   7 of PFL, pp. 33–169 (p. 109).

Chapter 2   The uncanny and its poetics

Some of the material in this chapter appears in different form in
Modernism and the European Unconscious, ed. Peter Collier and Judy
Davies (Manchester, Manchester University Press, 1990).

1 Sigmund Freud, 'The uncanny', in *Art and Literature*, ed. Albert
   Dickson (Harmondsworth, Penguin Books, 1985), vol. 14 of
   PFL, pp. 335–76.
2 Ibid., p. 339.
3 Ibid., p. 347.
4 Sigmund Freud, 'Three letters from Sigmund Freud to André
   Breton', in *Journal of the American Psychoanalytical Association*,
   21 (1973), pp. 127–34 [letter of 14 December 1932].
5 Theodor Adorno, 'Looking back on Surrealism', in *Notes to Literature*, vol. 1, ed. Rolf Tiedemann, trans. Shierry Weber Nicholsen
   (New York, Columbia University Press, 1991), pp. 86–90.
6 Freud, 'The uncanny', pp. 362–3.
7 Ibid., p. 372.
8 Hélène Cixous, 'Fiction and its phantoms: A reading of Freud's
   Das Unheimliche', in *New Literary History*, 7 (Spring, 1976),

pp. 525–48; see also Neil Hertz, 'Freud and the sandman', in *Textual Strategies: Perspectives in Post-Structuralist Criticism*, ed. Josué V. Harari (London, Methuen, 1980), pp. 296–321.

9   Jean-François Lyotard, 'The sublime and the avant-garde', in *The Lyotard Reader*, ed. Andrew Benjamin (Oxford, Blackwell, 1989), pp. 196–211 (pp. 204–6).

10   Ibid., p. 206. See also p. 208: 'The avant-gardist attempt inscribes the occurrence of a sensory now as what cannot be presented.'

11   André Breton, *What is Surrealism?: Selected Writings*, ed. Franklin Rosemont (London, Pluto Press, 1978), p. 195.

12   Michel Foucault, *This is not a Pipe* (Berkeley and London, University of California Press, 1983).

13   Sigmund Freud, 'From the history of an infantile neurosis (the "Wolf Man")', *Case Histories II*, ed. Angela Richards (Harmondsworth, Penguin Books, 1979), vol. 9 of PFL, pp. 227–366.

14   Ibid., pp. 243–4.

15   For a comprehensive and meticulously documented account, see Sarah Kofman, *The Childhood of Art: An Interpretation of Freud's Aesthetics* (New York, Columbia University Press, 1988).

16   Freud, 'Creative writers and daydreaming', in vol. 14 of PFL (see n. 1), pp. 129–41.

17   Freud, 'Psychopathic characters on the stage', in vol. 14 of PFL (see n. 1), pp. 121–7.

18   André Green, 'The double and the absent', in *Psychoanalysis, Creativity and Literature: A French-American Inquiry*, ed. Alan Roland (New York, Columbia University Press, 1978), pp. 271–92 (p. 283).

19   Jean Laplanche and Jean-Bertrand Pontalis, *The Language of Psychoanalysis*, trans. Daniel Lagache (London, The Hogarth Press and the Institute of Psycho-Analysis, 1973), p. 433.

20   Melanie Klein, 'Love, guilt and reparation', in *Love, Guilt and Reparation and Other Works, 1921–1945* (New York, Dell Publishing Company, 1975), pp. 306–43.

21   Sigmund Freud, 'Three essays on sexuality', in *On Sexuality*, ed. Angela Richards (Harmondsworth, Penguin Books, 1977), vol. 7 of PFL pp. 33–169 (p. 94).

Chapter 3   The vagaries of fantasy: Alfred Kubin's *The Other Side*

1   Sigmund Freud, 'Creative writers and daydreaming', in *Art and Literature*, ed. Albert Dickson (Harmondsworth, Penguin Books,

1985), vol. 14 of PFL, pp. 129–41 (p. 134).

2   Ibid.

3   Sigmund Freud, 'Psychopathic characters on the stage', in *Art and Literature* , ed. Albert Dickson (Harmondsworth, Penguin Books, 1985), vol. 14 of PFL, pp. 121–7.

4   Alfred Kubin, *The Other Side*, trans. Denver Lindley (London, Victor Gollancz, 1969 [first published as *Die andere Seite: Ein phantastischer Roman*, München, G. Müller, 1909]).

5   'Alfred Kubin's autobiography', in ibid., pp. 1– lxxviii, (xxxvii, xl).

6   Sigmund Freud,*The Interpretation of Dreams*, ed. James Strachey and Alan Tyson, rev. Angela Richards (Harmondsworth, Penguin Books, 1976), vol. 4 of PFL, p. 112. The original sentence reads '*der Schauplatz der Träume ein anderer ist*'. Freud traces the idea to G. T. Fechner.

7   Jacques Lacan, *The Ethics of Psychoanalysis 1959–1960: The Seminar of Jacques Lacan, Book VII*, ed. Jacques-Alain Miller, trans. Dennis Porter (London, Routledge and Tavistock Publications, 1992), p. 320.

8   Ibid., pp. 53–4. In his Ethics seminar, Lacan extensively discusses this term in relation to Freud's thought. He draws out the distinction between Freud's use of the terms *die Sache* and *das Ding*, the former being the perceived thing/object as the symbolic would have it, certain and reproducible, and the latter as the thing/object 'in its dumb reality' (p. 55). In Freud's *Project for a Scientific Psychology*, to which Lacan refers (pp. 35–42), there is a similar dividing of an 'understandable' aspect of the thing and a 'non-understood' one (Freud, 1895, pp. 383–4), a (symbolic) judgement undermined by the (real) 'perceptual complex', the sensory intake. For Lacan, the security of any 'thing' in its '*Sache*' aspect implies the same absorption in the mother for which object-relations psychology argues, being unaware that its categories of 'frustration, satisfaction and dependence' are imaginary categories, which lure the infant to attempt an incessant return to fusion with the 'maternal thing' (p. 67).

9   Samuel Taylor Coleridge, *Biographia Literaria* (London, J. M. Dent and Sons, 1947 [first published 1817]), p. 76, pp. 145–6.

10 Ibid., p. 145.

11 Sigmund Freud, 'Beyond the pleasure principle' , in *On Metapsychology: The Theory of Psychoanalysis*, ed. Angela Richards (Harmondsworth, Penguin Books, 1984), vol. 11 of PFL, pp. 269–338 (pp. 277–80).

Chapter 4   Maladies of the soul: the poetics of Julia Kristeva

1 Sigmund Freud, 'Creative writers and daydreaming', in *Art and Literature*, ed. Albert Dickson (Harmondsworth, Penguin Books, 1985), vol. 14 of PFL, pp. 129–41 (p. 132).

2 Julia Kristeva, *Black Sun: Depression and Melancholia*, trans. Leon S. Roudiez (New York, Columbia University Press 1989), p. 13.

3 Julia Kristeva, *New Maladies of the Soul*, trans. Ross Guberman (New York, Columbia University Press, 1995).

4 For Nerval's poem 'The disinherited' see *Black Sun*, pp. 140–1; Vaughan's phrase is in line 50 of his poem 'The Night', from Part 2 of his collection *Silex Scintillans*.

5 Kristeva's quotation is from Gérard de Nerval, 'Aurelia', in *Selected Writings*, trans. Geoffrey Wagner (Ann Arbor, University of Michigan Press, 1957), p. 130.

6 Julia Kristeva, *Powers of Horror: An Essay on Abjection*, trans. Leon S. Roudiez (New York, Columbia University Press, 1982).

7 Ibid., p. 12.

8 Sigmund Freud, 'Mourning and melancholia', in *On Metapsychology: The Theory of Psychoanalysis*, ed. Angela Richards (Harmondsworth, Penguin Books, 1984), vol. 11 of PFL, pp. 247–338 (p. 258).

9 Sigmund Freud, 'The Ego and the Id', in *On Metapsychology* (see preceding note), pp. 339–407 (p. 370).

10 Ibid.

11 Marguerite Duras, *La Maladie de la mort* (Paris, Minuit, 1982).

12 Kristeva's extract is from Marguerite Duras, *La Douleur* (Paris, POL, 1985), p. 57.

13 Sigmund Freud, 'Dostoevsky and parricide', in *Art and Literature* (see note 1), pp. 436–60.

14 Ibid., p. 447.

15 For a recent overview of borderline states, see Judith Feher Gurewich and Michael Tort (eds), *The Subject and the Self: Lacan and American Psychoanalysis* (Northvale, New Jersey, Jason Aronson Inc., 1996).

16 For the term 'Gracehoper' see James Joyce, *Finnegan's Wake* (London, Faber, 1975), p. 416.

17 For a discussion of André Green's term 'trans-narcissistic' see Elizabeth Wright, *Psychoanalytic Criticism: A Reappraisal* (Cambridge, Polity Press, 1998), p. 92.

18 See James Joyce, *Portrait of the Artist as a Young Man* (London, Jonathan Cape, 1950), p. 245: 'The artist, like the God of creation, remains within or behind or beyond or above his handiwork, invisible, refined out of existence, indifferent, paring his fingernails.'

Chapter 5   What is a discourse?

Some of the material in this chapter appears in different form in *The Edinburgh Encyclopedia of Continental Philosophy*, ed. Simon Glendinning (Edinburgh, Edinburgh University Press, 1999).

1 Ferdinand de Saussure, *Course in General Linguistics*, ed. Charles Bally and Albert Sechehaye, trans. Wade Baskin (London, Fontana/Collins, 1977), p. 113.

2 Roman Jakobson and Maurice Halle, *Fundamentals of Language* (Gravenhage, Mouton, 1960), p. 353.

3 Jacques Lacan, 'The mirror stage as formative of the function of the I as revealed in psychoanalytic experience', in *Écrits: A Selection*, trans. Alan Sheridan (London, Tavistock Publications, 1977), pp. 1–7.

4 Lacan, 'Agency of the letter in the unconscious of reason since Freud', in *Écrits*, pp. 147–78 (pp. 158, 160, 164).

5 Jacques Lacan, *Le Séminaire, Livre XVII: L'Envers de la psychanalyse, 1969/70*, ed. Jacques-Alain Miller (Paris, Seuil, 1991); see also Paul Verhaeghe, *The Woman Does Not Exist* (London and New York, Rebus – The Other Press, 1999), pp. 95–118; Bruce Fink, *The Lacanian Subject: Between Language and Jouissance* (Princeton, New Jersey, Princeton University Press, 1995), pp. 129–37.

6 Émile Benveniste, *Problems in General Linguistics* (Miami, Florida, University of Miami Press, 1971), pp. 206–9.

7 Sigmund Freud, 'Beyond the Pleasure Principle', in *On Metapsychology*, ed. Angela Richards (Harmondsworth, Penguin Books, 1984), vol. 11 of PFL, pp. 269–338.

8 Jacques Lacan, *Four Fundamental Concepts of Psychoanalysis*, ed. Jacques-Alain Miller, trans. Alan Sheridan (London, The Hogarth Press and the Institute of Psycho-Analysis, 1977), pp. 111–12.

9 William Wordsworth, 'Elegiac Stanzas: Suggested by a Picture of Peele Castle, in a Storm, Painted by Sir George Beaumont' (1805) [here reprinted from the Everyman edition of Wordsworth's *Shorter Poems*]:

I was thy neighbour once, thou rugged Pile!
Four summer weeks I dwelt in sight of thee:
I saw thee every day; and all the while
Thy Form was sleeping on a glassy sea.

So pure the sky, so quiet was the air!
So like, so very like, was day to day!
Whene'er I looked, thy Image still was there;
It trembled, but it never passed away.

How perfect was the calm! it seemed no sleep;
No mood, which season takes away, or brings:
I could have fancied that the mighty Deep
Was even the gentlest of all gentle things.

Ah! THEN, if mine had been the Painter's hand,
To express what then I saw; and add the gleam,
The light that never was, on sea or land,
The consecration and the Poet's dream;

I would have planted thee, thou hoary Pile,
Amid a world how different from this!
Beside a sea that could not cease to smile;
On tranquil land, beneath a sky of bliss.

Thou should'st have seemed a treasure-house divine
Of peaceful years; a chronicle of heaven; —
Of all the sunbeams that did ever shine,
The very sweetest had to thee been given.

A Picture had it been of lasting ease,
Elysian quiet, without toil or strife;
No motion but the moving tide, a breeze,
Or merely silent Nature's breathing life.

Such, in the fond illusion of my heart,
Such picture would I at that time have made:
And seen the soul of truth in every part,
A stedfast peace that might not be betrayed.

So once it would have been, – 'tis so no more;
I have submitted to a new control:

A power is gone, which nothing can restore;
A deep distress hath humanized my Soul.

Not for a moment could I now behold
A smiling sea, and be what I have been:
The feeling of my loss will ne'er be old;
This, which I know, I speak with mind serene.

Then, Beaumont, Friend! who would have been the Friend,
If he had lived, of Him whom I deplore,
This work of thine I blame not, but commend;
This sea in anger, and that dismal shore.

O 'tis a passionate Work! – yet wise and well,
Well chosen is the spirit that is here;
That Hulk which labours in the deadly swell,
This rueful sky, this pageantry of fear!

And this huge Castle, standing here sublime,
I love to see the look with which it braves,
Cased in the unfeeling armour of old time,
The lightning, the fierce wind, and trampling waves.

Farewell, farewell the heart that lives alone,
Housed in a dream, at distance from the Kind!
Such happiness, wherever it be known,
Is to be pitied, for 'tis surely blind.

But welcome fortitude, and patient cheer,
And frequent sights of what is to be borne!
Such sights, or worse, as are before me here. —
Not without hope we suffer and we mourn.

10 Immanuel Kant, 'Critique of aesthetic judgement', section 28, Book II of Part I in his *The Critique of Judgement*, trans. James Creed Meredith (Clarendon Press, Oxford, 1957), pp. 109–14.
11 Harold Bloom, *The Anxiety of Influence: A Theory of Poetry* (London and Oxford, Oxford University Press, 1975).
12 Jacques Lacan, 'Seminar on "The purloined letter"', *Yale French Studies*, 48 (1972), pp. 39–72.

Chapter 6   The indirections of desire: *Hamlet*

1   Jacques Lacan, 'Desire and the interpretation of desire in *Hamlet*', in *Literature and Psychoanalysis. The Question of Reading: Otherwise, Yale French Studies*, 55–6 (1977), pp. 11–52 (p.13).
2   The graphs are referred to in an editorial footnote in the English text because Lacan makes repeated allusion to them. For the full presentation of the graphs, see 'The subversion of the subject and the dialectic of desire in the Freudian unconscious', in *Écrits: A Selection*, trans. Alan Sheridan (London, Tavistock Publications, 1977), pp. 292–325 (pp. 312–16). In these graphs Lacan provides an evolving schema of the structures that operate in the constitution of the subject, with particular reference to its relation to language and the effects of the crystallizing out of elements within the unconscious. What these graphs illustrate is that, in being drawn into the symbolic, in being 'interpellated' (Althusser's term), the subject has to accept that it is not wholly defined from without. This implies that it must enter into the process of defining itself, and this involves engaging itself in the operations of the symbolic, the big Other. The first endeavour of the subject is to identify with the Other's desire (initially represented by the mother) because language, the code, is a means by which we, in pursuit of our desires, adjust our concepts to what exists. But language comes with a price. The subject's real is not met by language nor is that of other subjects nor is the Other's desire, the idealized coincidence of all these desires. The consequence of this encounter with language is the split subject (S), split between what can be signified and what cannot.

What is also produced by this process is the ego ideal (I (O)), the identification with the place from where we are being observed – from where we look upon ourselves so that we appear likeable. We are endeavouring to inhabit the gaze of the Other, admiring ourselves from that position. The ego ideal is an external point of identification conceived of as an authority dominating the ego. The neurotic (Hamlet) is not able to get out of this position of imagining himself observed; he is not able to turn being for the Other into being for himself (he cannot accept responsibility within himself for the Law).

Out of the subject's confrontation with the symbolic arises the problem of the subject's desire. Its symbolic identification remains at odds with its imaginary one because of the real leftover. Hence the subject is asking the question '*Che vuoi?*' 'What do you want (of me)?' The question the subject is really asking is 'What do you want me to want? What do I do with *d* (my desire)?' The subject wants to know what the Other's desire is so that it can form its identity around that desire. Through the recognition that the Other too is suffering from lack, is also castrated, the subject can learn to accept its own castration, a realization which prevents it from thinking itself totally alienated.

For Hamlet, as for the paradigmatic neurotic subject, this process of subject constitution has been interrupted because of the lack of a lack in the (m)Other. Lacan calls Hamlet 'the tragedy of desire', because Hamlet is unable to free himself from the desire of the (m)Other until he comes to the point of death.

3 Sigmund Freud, *The Interpretation of Dreams*, ed. James Strachey and Alan Tyson, rev. Angela Richards (Harmondsworth, Penguin Books, 1976), vol. 4 of PFL, pp. 366–8; Ernest Jones, *Hamlet and Oedipus* (London, Victor Gollancz, 1949).

4 Freud, ibid., p. 367.

5 Jones, ibid., pp. 22–3.

6 Lacan distinguishes between the real phallus (penis), the imaginary phallus (imputed to the mother's desire), and the symbolic phallus (the function of castration).

7 *Extimité* is Lacan's equivalent for the uncanny, expressing the impossibility of drawing a clear line between inside and outside, thus provoking horror and anxiety.

8 Sigmund Freud, *Totem and Taboo*, in *The Origins of Religion*, ed. Albert Dickson (Harmondsworth, Penguin Books, 1985), vol. 13 of PFL, pp. 43–224.

9 Lacan's three stages (castration, frustration and privation) correspond to Kierkegaard's three stages of coming into existence, the 'aesthetic', the 'ethical' and the 'religious'. For Kierkegaard: first, the aesthetic (feeling) stage is one in which the subject's spontaneous pursuit of delight produces a flight from selfhood that ends in despair; second, the ethical stage is one in which the subject unquestioningly allows itself to be guided by universal rule; and third, the 'religious' stage is reached when the subject takes up full responsibility for the law, if need be against the universal norm itself. (See Søren Kierkegaard, *A Kierkegaard Anthology*, ed. Robert Bretall, Princeton, New Jersey, Princeton University Press, 1946, pp. 96, 105–8, 129–34, 226–52.) This might be seen as a Lacanian dialectical advance from being over-

whelmed by the drive as it suffers the shock of primal repression, through being bound to the symbolic, to a mediation (*Aufhebung*) whereby real and symbolic are realigned.

Chapter 7   Inscribing the body politic: Robert Coover's *Spanking the Maid*

An earlier (shorter) version of this chapter appeared in *Textual Practice* 3 (1989), pp. 397–410 and in *Topoi*, 12 (1993), pp. 153–60.

1   Robert Coover, *Spanking the Maid* (New York, Grove Press, 1982).
2   Alan Friedman, 'Pleasure and pain', *New York Times Book Review*, 27 (June 1982), p. 20.
3   See Roland Barthes, *The Pleasure of the Text*, trans. Richard Miller (New York, Hill and Wang, 1975 [French original 1973]).
4   Sigmund Freud, 'A child is being beaten', in *On Pschopathology: Inhibitions, Symptoms and Anxiety*, ed. Angela Richards (Harmondsworth, Penguin Books,1979), vol. 10 of PFL, pp. 159–93.
5   Ibid., p. 170.
6   Ibid., p. 175.
7   Jacques Lacan, 'The function and field of speech and language in psychoanalysis', in *Écrits: A Selection*, trans. Alan Sheridan (London, Tavistock Publications,1977), p. 69.
8   Julia Kristeva, *Powers of Horror: An Essay on Abjection*, trans. Leon S. Roudiez (New York, Columbia University Press, 1982), p. 10. Though the abject is repugnant, the victim is helplessly fascinated by what hovers at its boundary, driven by the impulse to fuse the alienated 'I' and the Other (the symbolic) into an impossible whole, a coincidence of being, images and words.
9   Ibid., p. 8.
10   William Wordsworth, *The Prelude*, 1805, Book I, lines 350–6.
11   Barthes distinguishes texts of 'pleasure' (*plaisir*) from those of 'bliss' (translated from *jouissance*): 'Text of pleasure: the text that contents, fills, grants euphoria; the text that comes from culture and does not break with it is linked to a *comfortable* practice of reading. Text of bliss: the text that imposes a state of loss, the text that discomforts (perhaps to the point of a certain boredom), unsettles the reader's historical, cultural, psychological assumptions, the consistency of his taste, values, memories, brings to a crisis his relation with language' (*The Pleasure of the*

Text, p. 14; see note 3). Coover's text might thus rank as a text of the latter kind.

12 Fredric Jameson, *The Political Unconscious: Narrative as a Socially Symbolic Act* (London, Methuen, 1981).
13 Gilles Deleuze and Félix Guattari, *Anti-Oedipus: Capitalism and Schizophrenia*, trans. Robert Hurley, Mark Seem and Helen R. Lane (New York, Viking Press,1977), pp. 283–9.
14 Fredric Jameson, *Fables of Aggression: Wyndham Lewis, the Modernist as Fascist* (Berkeley, Los Angeles and London, University of California Press, 1979), p. 14.
15 D. H. Lawrence, *Studies in Classic American Literature* (Harmondsworth, Penguin Books, 1977), p. 89.
16 Michel Foucault, *The History of Sexuality: Vol. I, An Introduction* (Harmondsworth, Penguin Books, 1979), pp. 44–5.
17 Jean-Jacques Rousseau, *The Social Contract*, Book III, ch. 11.
18 Ibid., Book IV, ch. 2.

Chapter 8   What does Woman want?: *The Double Life of Véronique*

An earlier shorter version of this chapter appeared in *Psychoanalytic Psychology*, 10:3 (1993) pp. 481–6 and the *Australian Journal of Psychotherapy*, 14:1–2 (1995) pp. 13–19 under the joint authorship of Ellie Ragland and Elizabeth Wright. I would like to thank Danielle Bergeron for her insightful comments on this version.

1 Leonardo de la Fuente (producer) and Krzysztof Kieslowski (director), *La double vie de Véronique*; script by Krzysztof Kieslowski and Krzysztof Piesiewicz; music by Zbigniew Preisner (London, Gala Films, 1991).
2 E. T. A. Hoffmann, 'Councillor Krespel', in *Tales of Hoffmann*, trans. R. J. Hollingdale (Harmondsworth, Penguin Books, 1982), pp. 159–83; this forms the basis of the Antonia episode in Offenbach's opera *The Tales of Hoffmann*. Thomas Mann, 'Tristan', in *Stories of Three Decades* (London, Secker and Warburg, 1946 [German original 1902]) pp. 133–66.
3 Hoffmann, 'The sandman', in *Tales of Hoffmann*, pp. 85–125. Heinrich von Kleist, '*Über das Marionettentheater*', in *Werke und Briefe in vier Bänden, Bd. 4: Erzählungen, Gedichte, Anekdoten, Schriften*, ed. Siegfried Streller, Wolfgang Barthel, Anita Gotz and Rudolf Loch (Berlin and Weimar, Aufbau Verlag, 1978), pp. 473–80.

4   Jacques Lacan, 'The subversion of the subject and the dialectic of desire in the Freudian unconscious', in *Écrits: A Selection*, trans. A. Sheridan (London, Tavistock Publications, 1977), pp. 179–225 (p. 215).
5   Jacques Lacan, 'From love to the libido' [1973], in *The Four Fundamental Concepts of Psycho-Analysis*, ed. Jacques-Alain Miller, trans. Alan Sheridan (London, The Hogarth Press and the Institute of Psycho-Analysis, 1977), pp. 187–200 (p. 195).
6   Jacques Lacan, 'On *jouissance*', in *The Seminar of Jacques Lacan: On Feminine Sexuality. The Limits of Love and Knowledge, Book XX, Encore 1972–1973*, trans. Bruce Fink (New York and London, W. W. Norton and Co., 1998), pp. 9–13.

Chapter 9   What is a clinical 'case'?

1   Michael Horowitz, Paula Fuqua, Frank Summers and Harriet W. Meek, 'Clinical commentary XXII from America', *British Journal of Psychotherapy*, 14:3 (Spring, 1998), pp. 363–77.
2   Donald P. Spence, *The Rhetorical Voice of Psychoanalysis: Displacement of Evidence by Theory* (Cambridge, Massachusetts, Harvard University Press, 1994).
3   Jürgen Habermas, cited in Spence, ibid., p. 126.
4   Jacques Lacan, 'Science and truth', trans. Bruce Fink, *Newsletter of the Freudian Field*, 3:1–2, (Spring/Fall, 1989), pp. 4–29 (pp. 11–12).
5   For an illuminating account of Bachelard's thought, see Christopher Norris, 'Continental philosophy of science', in *The Edinburgh Encyclopedia of Continental Philosophy*, ed. Simon Glendinning (Edinburgh, Edinburgh University Press, 1999), pp. 402–15 (pp. 404–5).
6   Jacques Lacan, *Le Séminaire, Livre XVII: L'Envers de la psychanalyse, 1969–70* , ed. Jacques-Alain Miller (Paris, Seuil, 1991), p. 187.
7   William Wordsworth, 'Lines Written a Few Miles above Tintern Abbey, on Revisiting the Banks of the Wye During a Tour. July 13, 1798', lines 107–8.
8   David Tuckett, 'The conceptualization and communication of clinical facts in psychoanalysis', *International Journal of Psycho-Analysis*, 76:1 (1995), pp. 653–62 (pp. 657–8).

Chapter 10 The rhetoric of clinical discourse: *Dialogue with Sammy*

1   Joyce McDougall and Serge Lebovici, *Dialogue with Sammy: A Psychoanalytical Contribution to the Understanding of Child Psychosis* (London, Free Association Books, 1989).

2   In her postscript to the case McDougall gives an account of the analysis of Sammy's mother, which she undertook after Sammy's departure from Paris to Chicago and in which she explains how 'Sammy's image', as a 'phallic object for his mother', was 'deeply interwoven, with the mother's desire, her oral and phallic fantasies' (pp. 265–6).

3   Shoshana Felman, *Writing and Madness: (Literature/Philosophy/ Psychoanalysis)*, trans. Martha Noel Evans and Felman with the assistance of Brian Massumi (Ithaca, New York, Cornell University Press, 1985).

Chapter 11 The rhetoric of clinical management: Bion and Minuchin

1   Wilfred Bion, *Clinical Seminars and Other Works*, ed. Francesca Bion (London, Karnac Books, 1994).

2   See Goethe's sonnet *Natur und Kunst* ('Nature and Art'), particularly lines 13–14: '*In der Beschränkung zeigt sich erst der Meister, / Und das Gesetz nur kann uns Freiheit geben*'. ('Only with the acceptance of limit does Mastery show itself, And only Law can bestow freedom upon us'.) [my translation] In *Goethe: Selected Verse*, trans. David Luke (Harmondsworth, Penguin Books, 1964), p. 197.

3   Salvador Minuchin, *Families and Family Therapy* (London: Tavistock Publications, 1974).

4   Salvador Minuchin, Bernice L. Rosman, and Lester Baker, *Psychosomatic Families: Anorexia Nervosa in Context* (Cambridge, Massachusetts, and London, Harvard University Press, 1978); see also Tullio Maranhão, *Therapeutic Discourse and Socratic Dialogue* (Madison, University of Wisconsin Press, 1986), whose summary of the case I have found very helpful.

Chapter 12   Out of tune: Elfriede Jelinek's *The Piano Teacher*

An earlier version of this chapter appeared in *Paragraph*, 14:2 (1991).

1   See Roland Barthes, *The Pleasure of the Text*, trans. Richard Miller (New York, Hill and Wang, 1975 [French original 1973]); Wolfgang Iser, 'The reading process: A Phenomenological approach', in *Reader-Response Criticism: From Formalism to Post-Structuralism*, ed. Jane P. Tompkins (Baltimore, Johns Hopkins University Press, 1980), pp. 50–69; Toril Moi, *Sexual/Textual Politics: Feminist Literary Theory* (London, Methuen, 1985).

2   Marie Bonaparte, *The Life and Works of Edgar Allan Poe* (London, Imago, 1949).

3   Sigmund Freud, 'Leonardo da Vinci and a memory of his childhood', in *Art and Literature*, ed. Albert Dickson (Harmondsworth, Penguin Books 1985), vol. 14 of PFL, pp. 143–231.

4   Shoshana Felman, 'On reading poetry: Reflections on the limits and possibilities of psychoanalytical approaches', in *The Literary Freud*, ed. Joseph H. Smith (New Haven and London, 1980), pp. 119–48, see also the series of competitive readings in *The Purloined Poe: Lacan, Derrida, and Psychoanalytic Reading*, ed. John P. Muller and William J. Richardson (Baltimore, Johns Hopkins University Press, 1988) and *In Dora's Case: Freud – Hysteria – Feminism*, ed. Charles Bernheimer and Claire Kahane, (New York, Columbia University Press, 1985).

5   Elfriede Jelinek, *The Piano Teacher*, trans. Joachim Neugroschel (Serpent's Tail, London, 1989 [German original 1983]).

6   See Annegret Mahler-Bungers, 'Der Trauer auf der Spur: Zu Elfriede Jelineks *Die Klavierspielerin*', *Freiburger literaturpsychologische Gespräche*, vol. 7 (Würzburg, 1988), pp. 80–95. Mahler-Bungers provides a brilliantly persuasive reading which argues that the text, written in the present tense throughout, enacts the fixation of the central figure in a timeless maternal symbiosis, which forces her to disavow sexual difference. Mahler-Bungers wishes to preserve the notion of castration as a symbolic process from the mutilation scenarios enacted in the text. She reveals how the text incorporates snatches of the lyrics from Schubert's *Winterreise*, a song-cycle setting twenty-four poems by Wilhelm Müller which grieves for a 'lost object', she connects the omission of reference to certain lyrics with the failure

to mourn the absence and death of the feeble-minded father in the text. See also Hedwig Appelt, *Die leibhaftige Literatur: Das Phantasma und die Präsenz der Trauer der Frau in der Schrift* (Weinheim and Berlin, Quadriga, 1989), pp. 111–32, for a Lacanian reading.

7 Ernst Kohut, *The Analysis of the Self* (New York, International Universities Press, 1971).

8 See the scene of the wager in Goethe's *Faust*, I, especially lines 1699–1702:

Werd' ich zum Augenblicke sagen:
Verweile doch! du bist so schön!
Dann magst du mich in Fesseln schlagen,
Dann will ich gern zugrunde gehen.

(If to the fleeting hour I say
'Remain, so fair art thou, remain!'
Then bind me with your fatal chain,
For I will perish in that day.)

Faust: Part One, trans. Philip Wayne (Harmondsworth, Penguin Books, 1971), p. 87.

9 Terry Eagleton, *The Ideology of the Aesthetic* (Oxford, Basil Blackwell,1990), p. 28.

10 Ibid., p. 12.

11 Jacques Lacan, 'The function and field of speech and language in psychoanalysis', in *Écrits: A Selection*, trans. Alan Sheridan (London, Tavistock Publications, 1977), p. 104. Lacan was alluding to Kojève's lectures on Hegel, given in the 1930s: Alexandre Kojève, *Introduction to the Reading of Hegel: Lectures on the Phenomenology of the Spirit*, ed. Allan Bloom, trans. James H. Nichols, Jr. (Ithaca and London, Cornell University Press, 1969).

12 Julia Kristeva, *Powers of Horror: An Essay on Abjection*, trans. Leon S. Roudiez (New York, Columbia University Press, 1982), p. 2.

13 Ibid., p. 11.

14 Ibid., p. 4.

15 Ibid.

16 Jacques Lacan, '*Kant avec Sade*', in *Écrits* (Paris, Seuil, 1966), pp. 765–90.

17 Judith Feher Gurewich and Michael Tort (eds), *The Subject and*

the Self: Lacan and American Psychoanalysis (Northvale, New Jersey, Jason Aronson Inc., 1996), p. 38.

18 Jelinek, a Marxist and a member of the Austrian Communist Party in the 1980s, admits to a feeling of defeat when it comes to her literary engagement: 'My writing is probably too pessimistic and too decadent. That's why the left reacts to it with some suspicion. I don't blame them. I just don't write with optimism or revolutionary zeal, as one might expect of me.' [my translation]. See the interview by Georg Biron, '*Wahrscheinlich wäre ich ein Lustmörder*' ('I could very easily be a sex murderer'), *Die Zeit* (24 September1984), p. 47.

Conclusion

1 See Nicholas Royle, 'Nuclear piece: *Memoires* of *Hamlet* and the time to come', *Diacritics*, 20:1 (1990), pp. 39–55.
2 Roy Schafer, whose career has spanned both literature and psychoanalysis, urges that Freud's legacy be placed in the context of modern critical theory. He pleads for the need of a persuasive rhetoric for psychoanalytic writing as against the present neutered mode, which he describes as that of a 'genderless, raceless, classless, expert delivering a monologue that gives all the appearance of having been stripped of rhetorical ploys', as if closing itself against alternative readings, unlike Freud's texts with their destabilizing, self-deconstructive effects (such as his essay 'The uncanny'). See *Retelling a Life: Narration and Dialogue in Psychoanalysis* (New York, Basic Books), 1992, pp. 150–1.
3 Roland Barthes, *The Pleasure of the Text*, trans. Richard Miller (New York, Hill and Wang, 1975 [French original 1973]).
4 To that extent I agree here with Schafer, *Retelling a Life*, p. 184.
5 Shoshana Felman, *Writing and Madness: (Literature/Philosophy/Psychoanalysis)*, trans. Martha Noel Evans and the author (Ithaca, New York, Cornell University Press, 1985), p. 122, here citing Jacques Lacan, '*La Méprise du sujet de savoir*', *Scilicet*, 1 (1938), p. 32.
6 Felman, *Writing and Madness*, p. 127.

Bibliography

Adorno, Theodor, 'Looking back on Surrealism', in *Notes to Literature*, vol. 1, ed. Rolf Tiedemann, trans. Shierry Weber Nicholsen (New York, Columbia University Press, 1991), pp. 86–90.

Appelt, Hedwig, *Die leibhaftige Literatur: Das Phantasma und die Präsenz der Trauer der Frau in der Schrift* (Weinheim and Berlin, Quadriga, 1989).

Barthes, Roland, *The Pleasure of the Text*, trans. Richard Miller (New York, Hill and Wang, 1975) [French original 1973].

Benveniste, Émile, *Problems in General Linguistics* (Miami, Florida, University of Miami Press, 1971).

Bernheimer, Charles and Kahane, Claire (eds), *In Dora's Case: Freud – Hysteria – Feminism* (New York, Columbia University Press, 1985).

Bion, Wilfred, *Clinical Seminars and Other Works*, ed. Francesca Bion (London, Karnac Books, 1994).

Biron, Georg, '*Wahrscheinlich wäre ich ein Lustmörder*' ('I could very easily be a sex murderer'), *Die Zeit* (24 September 1984), p. 47.

Bloom, Harold, *The Anxiety of Influence: A Theory of Poetry* (London and Oxford, Oxford University Press, 1975).

Bonaparte, Marie, *The Life and Works of Edgar Allan Poe* (London, Imago, 1949).

Booth, Wayne C., *The Rhetoric of Fiction* (Chicago and London, Chicago University Press, 1961).

Breton, André, *What is Surrealism?: Selected Writings*, ed. Franklin Rosemont (London, Pluto Press, 1978).

Brooks, Cleanth, *The Well-Wrought Urn: Studies in the Structure of Poetry*, (London, Methuen, 1968) [first published 1947].

Chomsky, Noam, *Aspects of the Theory of Syntax* (Cambridge, Massachusetts, MIT Press, 1965).

——, *The Logical Structure of Linguistic Theory* (New York and London, Plenum Press, 1975).

Cixous, Hélène, 'Fiction and its phantoms: A reading of Freud's *Das Unheimliche*', in *New Literary History*, 7 (Spring, 1976), pp. 525–48.

Coleridge, Samuel Taylor, *Biographia Literaria* (London, J. M. Dent and Sons 1947) [first published 1817].

Coover, Robert, *Spanking the Maid* (New York, Grove Press, 1982).

Deleuze, Gilles and Guattari, Félix, *Anti-Oedipus: Capitalism and Schizophrenia*, trans. Robert Hurley, Mark Seem and Helen R. Lane (New York, Viking Press, 1977).

Derrida, Jacques, *The Postcard: From Socrates to Freud and Beyond*, trans. Alan Bass (Chicago and London, Chicago University Press, 1987) [French original 1980].

Duras, Marguerite, *La Maladie de la mort* (Paris, Minuit, 1982).

——, *La Douleur* (Paris, POL, 1985).

Eagleton, Terry, *The Ideology of the Aesthetic* (Oxford, Blackwell, 1990).

Ellmann, Maud, *Psychoanalytic Literary Criticism* (London and New York, Longman, 1994).

Felman, Shoshana, 'To open the question', *Literature and Psychoanalysis. The Question of Reading: Otherwise*, in *Yale French Studies*, 55–6 (1997), pp. 5–10.

——, *Writing and Madness: (Literature/ Philosophy/ Psychoanalysis)*, trans. Martha Noel Evans and Felman with the assistance of Brian Massumi (Ithaca, New York, Cornell University Press, 1985).

——, 'On reading poetry: Reflections on the limits and possibilities of psychoanalytical approaches', in *The Literary Freud*, ed. Joseph H. Smith (New Haven and London, 1980), pp. 119–48.

Fink, Bruce, *The Lacanian Subject: Between Language and Jouissance* (Princeton, New Jersey, Princeton University Press, 1995).

Foucault, Michel, *The History of Sexuality: Vol. I, An Introduction* (Harmondsworth, Penguin Books, 1979).

——, *This is not a Pipe* (Berkeley and London, University of California Press, 1983).

Friedman, Alan, 'Pleasure and pain', *New York Times Book Review*, 27 (June 1982), p. 20.

Freud, Sigmund, *Project for a Scientific Psychology*, standard Edition, vol 1, trans. James Strachey (The Hogarth Press and the Institute of Psycho-Analysis, 1978 [1895]), pp. 283–397.

——, 'Three letters from Sigmund Freud to André Breton', *Journal of the American Psychoanalytical Association*, 21 (1973), pp. 127–34 [written 1932].

Freud, Sigmund, The Pelican Freud Library [PFL], 14 vols, ed. James Strachey, Alan Tyson, Angela Richards and Albert Dickson, trans. James Strachey (Harmondsworth, Penguin Books, 1976–85).

——, *The Interpretation of Dreams*, ed. James Strachey and Alan Tyson, rev. Angela Richards (Harmondsworth, Penguin Books, 1976), vol. 4 of PFL.

——, 'Three essays on sexuality', in *On Sexuality: Three Essays on the Theory of Sexuality and Other Works*, ed. Angela Richards (Harmondsworth, Penguin Books, 1977), vol. 7 of PFL, pp. 33–169.

——, 'A child is being beaten', in *On Psychopathology: Inhibitions, Symptoms and Anxiety*, ed. Angela Richards (Harmondsworth, Penguin Books, 1979), vol. 10 of PFL, pp. 159–93.

——, 'From the history of an infantile neurosis (the "Wolf Man")', *Case Histories II*, ed. Angela Richards (Harmondsworth, Penguin Books, 1979), vol. 9 of PFL, pp. 227–366.

——, 'Mourning and melancholia', In *On Metapsychology: The Theory of Psychoanalysis*, ed. Angela Richards (Harmondsworth, Penguin Books, 1984), vol. 11 of PFL, pp. 247–268.

——, 'Beyond the pleasure principle', in *On Metapsychology: The Theory of Psychoanalysis*, ed. Angela Richards (Harmondsworth, Penguin Books, 1984), vol. 11 of PFL, pp. 269–338.

——, 'The ego and the id', in *On Metapsychology: The Theory of Psychoanalysis*, ed. Angela Richards (Harmondsworth, Penguin Books, 1984), vol. 11 of PFL, pp. 339–407.

——, 'Totem and taboo', in *The Origins of Religion: Totem and Taboo, Moses and Monotheism, and Other Works*, ed. Albert Dickson (Harmondsworth, Penguin Books, 1985), vol. 13 of PFL, pp. 43–224.

——, 'Psychopathic characters on the stage', in *Art and Literature*, ed. Albert Dickson (Harmondsworth, Penguin Books, 1985), vol. 14 of PFL, pp. 121–7.

——, 'Creative writers and daydreaming', in *Art and Literature*, ed. Albert Dickson, (Harmondsworth, Penguin Books, 1985), vol. 14 of PFL, pp. 129–41.

——, 'Leonardo da Vinci and a memory of his childhood', in *Art and Literature*, ed. Albert Dickson (Harmondsworth, Penguin Books, 1985), vol. 14 of PFL, pp. 143–231.

——, 'The uncanny', in *Art and Literature*, ed. Albert Dickson (Harmondsworth, Penguin Books, 1985), vol. 14 of PFL, pp. 335–76.

——, 'Dostoevsky and parricide', in *Art and Literature*, ed. Albert Dickson (Harmondsworth, Penguin Books, 1985), vol. 14 of PFL, pp. 436–60.

Green, André, 'The double and the absent', in *Psychoanalysis, Creativity and Literature: A French-American Inquiry*, ed. Alan Roland (New York, Columbia University Press, 1978), pp. 271–92.

Gurewich, Judith Feher and Tort, Michael (eds), *The Subject and the Self: Lacan and American Psychoanalysis* (Northvale, New Jersey: Jason Aronson Inc., 1996).

Hertz, Neil, 'Freud and the sandman', in *Textual Strategies: Perspectives in Post-Structuralist Criticism*, ed. Josué V. Harari (London, Methuen, 1980), pp. 296–321.

Hoffmann, E. T. A., 'The sandman' and 'Councillor Krespel', in *Tales of Hoffmann*, trans. R. J. Hollingdale (Harmondsworth, Penguin Books, 1982), pp. 85–125, 159–83.

Horowitz, Michael, Fuqua, Paula, Summers, Frank and Meek, Harriet W., 'Clinical commentary XXII from America', *British Journal of Psychotherapy*, 14:3 (Spring, 1998), pp. 363–77.

Iser, Wolfgang, 'The reading process: a phenomenological approach', in *Reader-Response Criticism: From Formalism to Post-Structuralism*, ed. Jane P. Tompkins (Baltimore, Johns Hopkins University Press, 1980), pp. 50–69.

Jakobson, Roman and Halle, Maurice, *Fundamentals of Language* (Gravenhage, Mouton, 1960).

Jameson, Fredric, *Fables of Aggression: Wyndham Lewis, the Modernist as Fascist* (Berkeley, Los Angeles and London, University of California Press, 1979).

——, *The Political Unconscious: Narrative as a Socially Symbolic Act* (London, Methuen, 1981).

Jelinek, Elfriede, *The Piano Teacher*, trans. Joachim Neugroschel (London, Serpent's Tail, 1989) [German original 1983].

Jones, Ernest, *Hamlet and Oedipus* (London, Victor Gollancz, 1949).

Joyce, James, *Finnegan's Wake* (London, Faber, 1975) [first published 1939].

——, *Portrait of the Artist as a Young Man* (London, Jonathan Cape, 1950) [first published 1916].

Kierkegaard, Søren, *A Kierkegaard Anthology*, ed. Robert Bretall (Princeton, New Jersey, Princeton University Press, 1946).

Klein, Melanie, 'Love, guilt and reparation', in *Love, Guilt and Reparation and Other Works, 1921–1945* (New York, Dell Publishing Company, 1975), pp. 306–43.

Kleist, Heinrich von, '*Über das Marionettentheater*', in *Werke und Briefe in vier Bänden, Bd. 4: Erzählungen, Gedichte, Anekdoten, Schriften*, ed. Siegfried Streller, Wolfgang Barthel, Anita Gotz and Rudolf Loch (Berlin and Weimar, Aufbau Verlag, 1978), pp. 473–80.

Kofman, Sarah, *The Childhood of Art: An Interpretation of Freud's Aesthetics* (New York, Columbia University Press, 1988).

Kohut, Ernst, *The Analysis of the Self* (New York, International Universities Press, 1971).

Kojève, Alexandre, *Introduction to the Reading of Hegel: Lectures on the Phenomenology of the Spirit*, ed. Allan Bloom, trans. James H. Nichols, Jr. (Ithaca and London, Cornell University Press, 1969).

Kristeva, Julia, *Powers of Horror: An Essay on Abjection*, trans. Leon S. Roudiez (New York, Columbia University Press, 1982).

——, *Black Sun: Depression and Melancholia*, trans. Leon S. Roudiez (New York, Columbia University Press, 1989).

——, *New Maladies of the Soul*, trans. Ross Guberman (New York, Columbia University Press, 1995).

Kubin, Alfred, *The Other Side*, trans. Denver Lindley (London, Victor Gollancz, 1969) [first published as *Die andere Seite: Ein phantastischer Roman*, München: G. Müller, 1909].

Lacan, Jacques, '*La Méprise du sujet de savoir*', *Scilicet*, 1 (1938), p. 32.

——, '*Kant avec Sade*', in *Écrits* (Paris, Seuil 1966), pp. 765–90.

——, '*La science et la vérité*', in *Écrits* (Paris, Seuil, 1966), pp. 855–77.

——, 'Seminar on "The purloined letter"', *Yale French Studies*, 48 (1972), pp. 39–72.

—— 'The mirror stage as formative of the function of the I as revealed in psychoanalytic experience', in *Écrits: A Selection*, trans. Alan Sheridan (London, Tavistock Publications, 1977), pp. 1–7.

——, 'The function and field of speech and language in psychoanalysis', in *Écrits: A Selection*, pp. 30–113.

——, 'Agency of the letter in the unconscious of reason since Freud', in *Écrits: A Selection*, pp. 147–78.

——, 'The subversion of the subject and the dialectic of desire in the Freudian unconscious', in *Écrits: A Selection*, pp. 292–325.

——, *Four Fundamental Concepts of Psychoanalysis*, ed. Jacques-Alain Miller, trans. Alan Sheridan (London, The Hogarth Press and the Institute of Psycho-Analysis, 1977).

——, 'From love to the libido' [1973], in *The Four Fundamental Concepts of Psycho-Analysis*, pp. 187–200.

——, 'Desire and the interpretation of desire in *Hamlet*', in *Literature and Psychoanalysis. The Question of Reading: Otherwise. Yale French Studies*, 55–6 (1977), pp. 11–52 [originally from the final three sessions of *Le Désir et son interpretation: Séminaire VI*, ed. Jacques-Alain Miller, *Ornicar?*, 24 (1981), pp. 7–31; 25 (1982), pp. 13–36; 26–7 (1983), pp. 7–44].

——, 'Science and truth', trans. Bruce Fink, *Newsletter of the Freudian Field*, 3:1–2 (Spring/Fall, 1989), pp. 4–29.

——, *Le Séminaire, Livre XVII: L'Envers de la psychanalyse, 1969/70*, ed. Jacques-Alain Miller (Paris, Seuil, 1991).

——, *The Ethics of Psychoanalysis 1959–1960: The Seminar of Jacques Lacan, Book VII*, ed. Jacques-Alain Miller, trans. Dennis Porter (London, Routledge and Tavistock Publications, 1992).

——, 'On *jouissance*', in *The Seminar of Jacques Lacan: On Feminine Sexuality. The Limits of Love and Knowledge, Book XX, Encore 1972–1973*, trans. Bruce Fink (New York and London, W. W. Norton and Co., 1998), pp. 9–13.

Laplanche, Jean and Pontalis, Jean-Bertrand, *The Language of Psychoanalysis*, trans. Daniel Lagache (London, The Hogarth Press and the Institute of Psycho-Analysis, 1973) [French original 1967].

Lawrence, D. H., *Studies in Classic American Literature* (Harmondsworth, Penguin Books, 1977).

Lyotard, Jean-François, 'The sublime and the avant-garde', in *The Lyotard Reader*, ed. Andrew Benjamin (Oxford, Blackwell, 1989), pp. 196–211.

McDougall, Joyce and Lebovici, Serge, *Dialogue with Sammy: A Psychoanalytical Contribution to the Understanding of Child Psychosis* (London, Free Association Books, 1989).

Mahler-Bungers, Annegret, '*Der Trauer auf der Spur: Zu Elfriede Jelineks Die Klavierspielerin*', *Freiburger literaturpsychologische Gespräche*, vol. 7 (Würzburg, 1988), pp. 80–95.

Mann, Thomas, 'Tristan', in *Der Tod in Venedig und andere Erzählungen* (Frankfurt am Main and Hamburg, Fischer Bücherei, 1971), pp. 69–103.

Maranhão, Tullio, *Therapeutic Discourse and Socratic Dialogue*, (Madison, University of Wisconsin Press, 1986).

Minuchin, Salvador, *Families and Family Therapy* (London, Tavistock Publications, 1974).

——, Rosman, Bernice L. and Baker, Lester, *Psychosomatic Families: Anorexia Nervosa in Context* (Cambridge, Massachusetts, and London, Harvard University Press, 1978).

Moi, Toril, *Sexual/Textual Politics: Feminist Literary Theory* (London, Methuen, 1985).

Norris, Christopher, 'Continental philosophy of science', in *The Edinburgh Encyclopedia of Continental Philosophy*, ed. Simon Glendinning (Edinburgh, Edinburgh University Press, 1999), pp. 402–15.

Ransom, John Crowe, *The New Criticism* (Norfolk, Virginia, New Directions, 1941) [first published 1938].

Royle, Nicholas, 'Nuclear piece: *Memoires* of *Hamlet* and the time to come', *Diacritics*, 20:1 (1990), pp. 39–55.

Saussure, Ferdinand de, *Course in General Linguistics*, ed. Charles Bally and Albert Sechehaye, trans. Wade Baskin (London, Fontana/Collins, 1977) [first published 1916].

Schafer, Roy, *Retelling a Life: Narration and Dialogue in Psychoanalysis* (New York, Basic Books, 1992), pp. 150–1.

Spence, Donald P., *The Rhetorical Voice of Psychoanalysis: Displacement of Evidence by Theory* (Cambridge, Massachusetts, Harvard University Press, 1994).

Tuckett, David, 'The conceptualization and communication of clinical facts in psychoanalysis', *International Journal of Psycho-Analysis*, 76:1 (1995), pp. 653–62.

Verhaeghe, Paul, *The Woman Does Not Exist* (London and New York, Rebus – The Other Press, 1999).

Wright, Elizabeth, *Psychoanalytic Criticism: A Reappraisal* (Cambridge, Polity Press, 1998).

Index